"Zach offers a practical guide to church polity leadership, especially for pastors seeking to lovingly shepherd their congregations well through change. His heartfelt stories and lived experience give depth to each principle, allowing readers to see how faithful leadership is lived out in real ministry. Humble, clear, and deeply encouraging, this book will bless and strengthen every pastor who desires to lead with grace and wisdom."

—**Jon Martin**, Chief Strategy Officer, Mississippi Baptist Convention Board

"The concern for biblical polity in the local church has increasingly grown as a concern in recent years in Baptist churches. This is especially true concerning the nature of pastors and elders in a church. The questions of 'Who should be a pastor?' or 'How many elders should a church have?' are the impetus for many books and articles. In this volume Zach Kilpatrick adds a helpful and practical word to that conversation by addressing how to lead a church to evaluate and change their polity. Anyone looking to engage in a change to a plurality of elders will find this book essential to that task."

—**W. Madison Grace II**, Dean, School of Theology, Southwestern Baptist Theological Seminary

"Leading change in any long-standing organization is never easy. It requires vision, courage, patience, and much wisdom to do it successfully. Zach Kilpatrick has written a book to aid us all in a much-needed area of change in local churches. Moving to a plural elder polity is a return to a biblical model that strengthens and blesses those churches in significant ways. I am grateful for this book and grateful for the example and wisdom that Zach has demonstrated in his own context. This book will serve current and future churches in restoring what has been lost in many places. I hope you read it and follow Zach's suggestions. We are all indebted to him."

—**Greg Belser**, Senior Pastor, Morrison Heights Baptist Church

"Born out of a pastor's heart and forged in the trenches of faithful local ministry, Zach Kilpatrick's work, *Shifting Polity*, offers a practical guide for pastors and church leaders seeking to transition from a single-pastor model to a biblically grounded plurality of elders. So often these conversations stay at the theoretical and hypothetical. Kilpatrick offers a biblically saturated framework that is drenched with lived patience, wisdom, and humility. I pray that this timely resource will strengthen and encourage healthier patterns of pastoral leadership for decades to come."

—**David Eldridge**, Senior Pastor,
Dawson Memorial Baptist Church

"Zach Kilpatrick's careful study, teaching, and leadership of moving from a single pastor model of church leadership to multiple elders is a great example for other pastors. His advice is biblical and practical. It's clear, Zach loves Mt. Zion Baptist Church. I have loved watching Zach, mainly from the other side of the world, as he introduced this transition over the last few years. In three decades of cross-cultural church planting in Central Asia, I have learned to look for new missionaries who are sent out from healthy local churches. They love the Bride of Christ not only from their time in the word but from how they have personally experienced the local church. We most easily replicate what we have known first-hand. I'd give particular attention to any potential missionaries from this church. They would be coming from a great environment, where their elders have sought to equip 'the saints for the work of ministry' and 'to build up the body of Christ' (Ephesians 4:12)."

—**Winfield Scott**, International Mission Leader

Shifting Polity

Shifting Polity

A Blueprint for Helping "Traditional" Churches Embrace the Tradition of Elder Polity

ZACHARY T. KILPATRICK

Foreword by Phil A. Newton

WIPF & STOCK · Eugene, Oregon

SHIFTING POLITY
A Blueprint for Helping "Traditional" Churches Embrace the Tradition of Elder Polity

Wipf & Stock
An Imprint of Wipf and Stock Publishers
199 W. 8th Ave., Suite 3
Eugene, OR 97401

www.wipfandstock.com

PAPERBACK ISBN: 979-8-3852-5512-2
HARDCOVER ISBN: 979-8-3852-5513-9
EBOOK ISBN: 979-8-3852-5514-6

VERSION NUMBER 02/12/26

To my gracious and patient wife, Amanda, and my beautiful children, Chip, Addy, Chase, Jett, and Hope. I love you more than you know.

To all the saints of Mt. Zion Baptist Church. Without your love for God and his word, this book would not have been possible. You are a gift to me.

"So I exhort the elders among you . . . shepherd the flock of God that is among you, exercising oversight, not under compulsion, but willingly, as God would have you; not for shameful gain, but eagerly; not domineering over those in your charge, but being examples to the flock. And when the chief Shepherd appears, you will receive the unfading crown of glory."

—1 Peter 5:1–4

Contents

Illustrations

Foreword

YEARS AGO, I BEGAN a twenty-or-so hour journey to an Asian city, where I'd meet up with a few friends to teach on church leadership. I had been briefed that the pastors who planned to attend lived under constant scrutiny by authorities unfriendly toward the gospel. These pastors weighed on my mind as I flew the long hours, reading through my notes, and praying that I might be able to communicate well enough through translators to help them frame a biblical polity in their churches. After navigating a couple of airports where I had never been and arriving at my destination, I waited for a local brother I'd never met and who couldn't hold up a sign with my name due to security reasons. Finally, our eyes connected. We quickly headed for his car, away from curious eyes, and into the city of millions, where I'd spend a week teaching and interacting with pastors.

We had unforgettable meals together, sweet fellowship, and warm-hearted times of discussing God's word. Yet, a burden grew in my heart. I stared at the faces of these men singing Christian hymns, listening to Christian teaching, and drinking tea together during breaks. I realized some of the brothers would likely face imprisonment for their faithfulness as shepherds to their flocks. And maybe soon.

What struck me toward the end of the week with these amazingly joyful pastors was just how important church polity was in their setting. If their congregations depended upon one man to shepherd them instead of a plurality of elders teaching, shepherding, and caring for the flock, the congregation would be shepherdless if that one man was arrested. No one would be present to pastor them through the difficulties in living for Christ amid persecution. No one would be there to teach them about living in Christ. No one would counsel them in struggles with sin or comfort them in loss. More than ever, I understood polity could not be treated as a take-it-or-leave-it *program* for the church. Biblical church polity with plural elder leadership within congregational government meant the health and survival of a congregation.

A few years ago, I met Zach Kilpatrick. He told me that he pastored in Brookhaven, Mississippi, and was leading his church toward shifting their polity to plural elder congregationalism. My heart leaped! My first pastorate was about forty-five minutes from his church. I knew nothing about elder plurality among Baptists at that stage, but in reflection forty years later, I realized that leading them toward this massive polity shift would be rather earth-shattering in that part of the country. Zach and I kept in touch. He updated me on the progress of teaching his church about biblical polity, their congregational discussion, and the positive vote to change their polity. I imagine I let loose with a good "Hallelujah!" when the call ended. Why my elation?

Plural elder leadership among Baptists had been the norm with many Baptist churches on both sides of the Atlantic until sometime in the nineteenth century. Our forefathers saw it as necessary for gospel flourishing in their churches. But some key figures more influenced by political democracy than biblical congregationalism slowly turned most Baptists away from the biblical teaching on polity. It didn't happen overnight. It took over a century to tear away this foundational polity evident in Baptist confessions of faith. But it happened.

Thankfully, over the past three decades, Baptists have recovered what so many of our forebears practiced: lively congregationalism led by a plurality of godly elders who shepherded the church. Zach's study of Scripture and influence through pastors who've led their churches to embrace biblical polity (and I will say, historic

Baptist polity), has borne sweet fruit in Brookhaven, Mississippi. That's why I'm happy to commend his book *Shifting Polity* as a helpful guide for other pastors, leaders, and churches shifting their polity to align with God's word.

I've had countless conversations with brothers wanting to lead their churches in shifting polity but didn't know where to start or how to bring it along. That's where Zach's book serves the church. While giving some of the biblical and confessional rationale for plural elder leadership in a congregational government, he spends most of his work guiding pastors to gently, graciously, and steadily lead their churches to understand, approve, and implement elder plurality in their polity. You'll feel his warmth and pastoral gentleness in these pages. You'll also see his intentionality to lead the church to conform to the revelation of Holy Scripture. Plus, you'll find a friend ready to offer counsel in how to shift polity while shepherding the flock. *Shifting Polity* provides guidance from a faithful pastor who loves Christ's church and longs to see the gospel flourish in and through these congregations.

Phil A. Newton, PhD
Director of Pastoral Care and Mentoring
for The Pillar Network
Retired Lead Pastor
Visiting Professor of Pastoral Theology
at Southeastern Baptist Theological Seminary
Author of *Elders in the Life of the Church*
and *Mending the Nets: Rethinking Church Leadership*

Abbreviations

1 Cor	1 Corinthians
1 Pet	1 Peter
1 Tim	1 Timothy
Col	Colossians
Eph	Ephesians
Exod	Exodus
FAQ	Frequently Asked Questions
Heb	Hebrews
Jer	Jeremiah
MZBC	Mt. Zion Baptist Church
PAC	Pastoral Assessment Committee
Q&A	Question and Answer Sessions
Rom	Romans
RONR	Robert's Rules of Order, Newly Revised
SBC	Southern Baptist Convention

Introduction

FINDING REAL HOPE

"For every five pastors, one leaves pastoral ministry—not because of moral failure, retirement, or lack of faith—but because of burnout."[1] This brutal truth is staggering, yet it is only one of the significant challenges facing church leaders today—challenges like biblical illiteracy, theological shallowness, and declining membership.

I believe much of this is because pastors often have to make difficult decisions about what *not* to do. They only have so many hours and so many hands, so they are required to make difficult decisions, such as, do I neglect meeting one-on-one for counseling or sermon preparation? Will I invest in a struggling marriage or in a committee that needs guidance? Should I focus on equipping young leaders or providing direction to the staff?

I believe a root problem contributing to these issues is the leadership structure of our churches. Many churches are using a single-pastor model,[2] while Scripture indicates that the work of shepherding a church is a job for more than one person.[3] If you are

1. Sullivan, "Debunking the Myths," para. 10.

2. This is the term I use to refer to a church that only has one recognized pastor. He is tasked with doing all the pastoral work of leading, preaching, guiding, equipping, and congregational care alone.

3. Throughout the book, I will refer to this model of having more than one pastor in an individual church as a plural elder model. I believe this is the model seen in the churches in the New Testament.

reading this book, you can likely identify with these struggles and might be seeking a better model.

Perhaps what you need is encouragement and a plan to help move a church from the single pastor model, where one pastor or elder does all the shepherding alone, to a plural elder model, where multiple pastors, or elders, shepherd a church together.[4]

It is my prayer that this book will serve that purpose. I have been where you are. I was in my mid-thirties, pastoring a rural, established congregational Southern Baptist church with a single-pastor polity.[5] I desperately wanted the church to adopt a plural elder model, but I was terrified of the stories of church splits, dissension, and disunity that I had heard.

Those fears brought to mind another time in my life when I faced a mixture of excitement and uncertainty: cliff jumping.

I vividly remember standing on top of a rock high above Smith Lake in Northern Alabama, preparing to jump. I felt a mix of adventure and self-preservation; my heart said, "Go for it," but my mind screamed, "Don't do it!" I desired to take that first step and jump, but every instinct I had pressed me not to.

Many of you share those same feelings about leading this change. You deeply desire to take that first step and to see the church become healthier by adopting a new polity. However, you're also terrified of what will happen if you do.

One thing that most people don't see about cliff jumping is that it requires a lot of preparation. Leading a change of this nature does, too. Let me share about the difference that can make.

4. Throughout this book, I will use the terms "pastor" and "elder" interchangeably. I believe they are synonyms for the same office in the local church, the office of pastor/elder/overseer. For more, see Strauch, *Biblical Eldership*, 31–34.

5. The term polity refers to the type of government or leadership structure of a church.

EMBRACING A REALISTIC TIMELINE

Before jumping, I studied the lake's depth, the cliff's position, the proper way to enter the water, and more. These things allowed me to enter the water safely.

Similarly, before attempting to lead this change, you will need to undertake considerable work. This is not a quick fix for a hurting church but a multi-year commitment to leading towards a healthier change.

This transition process will likely take between two and five years, depending on your specific context. It will require a significant amount of time and energy, and it may still seem unattainable.

However, it is not. It can be done, even in a church like the one you are in, and in the end, it will be well worth the effort. Let me tell you how I know these things.

FOLLOWING REAL EXPERIENCE

I can confidently say this can be done in your context because I have seen it in a similar church with my own eyes. I was able to lead Mt. Zion Baptist Church (MZBC)—a 198-year-old church—to make this transition. After spending the requisite time and capital, the church made this transition joyfully, with over 95 percent of the congregation voting in favor of the change.

I can also speak from experience about the work being worth it. I have experienced the refreshment that comes with serving alongside other pastors. I have felt the relief of not having all the burden of pastoral ministry on my shoulders. Moreover, I have witnessed the difference it makes in a congregation. How the increase in leadership, guidance, mentoring, equipping, and teaching profoundly—and positively—impacts the lives of God's people.

Now, I would like to utilize my experience—and the experience of other similar churches—to help you achieve the same goal in the church where you serve.

OFFERING REAL HELP

You already possess the biblical conviction to begin this change, but like a man at the edge of a cliff, fear and self-preservation are keeping you from taking that first step. What you desire is a plan, a strategy, something that can give you confidence to lead this process.

That is where this book comes in. It is intended to provide a comprehensive and scripturally honoring blueprint for leading a change in polity. A blueprint proven in a real-world church, much like the one you are serving in. A clear plan based on other churches in similar contexts that have successfully made this same transition.

This book does more than offer hope. It includes a five-phase plan proven in established churches. This plan includes guidance on assessing the church's readiness[6] (chapter 1) and ways to educate them about biblical leadership and the benefits of this new system (chapters 2–3). It also includes steps for casting a clear vision (chapter 4), a plan for utilizing others to lead this change (chapter 5), and detailed plans for properly implementing this new polity (chapter 6).

No matter where you are in the process, my prayer is that the biblical principles, practical wisdom, and personal experiences shared in the following chapters will guide you to the next step. That they help you to find yourself among a council of elders, shepherding a church that is much more biblically literate, theologically deep, and spiritually healthy. And I pray that they will allow you to find freedom from the burnout and exhaustion that many pastors face.

This book is not theoretical for me. I have lived it firsthand and seen the difference this transition makes. I believe the church you are pastoring deserves healthy and comprehensive pastoral leadership by a council of qualified men.

If you are willing to commit to the patient and purposeful task of leading this change, then this book will provide you with the tools and timelines you need to make it happen. If you're ready to take that first step, then turn to chapter 1!

6. This is one of the most crucial steps in this process. As you will see in chapter 1, deciding to move forward at the wrong time can be devastating on the possibility of leading this change.

1

Evaluating Timing

Finding the Right Starting Place

Timing is everything.

—Modern Proverb

When I was a sophomore in college, there was a day that changed my life forever. I saw the most beautiful lady I had ever seen. I eventually asked her to be my girlfriend, to which she replied, "No."

Obviously, that was not the response I expected (or desired). I asked her five more times over the next five months, and each time she gave the same answer. However, she did eventually say yes, and we have now been happily married for seventeen years.

What made the difference? Did I ask in a different way? Did someone else ask on my behalf? No, each time it was the same question from the same person. The thing that changed was the timing.

From this experience, I learned a critical lesson: proper timing is invaluable!

This is true when it comes to relationships, but it is also true when leading a church to make a change in polity. If you are seeking to lead a change in polity, it is essential that you identify the proper timing and then progress through the process at an appropriate pace.

This chapter is specifically designed to help you identify the right time to begin leading this change in your local church and to decipher the speed at which you can move once you do. These things—referred to as the starting place and moving pace—are different for every church but are discernible through proper investigation.

In this chapter, we will explore the following factors: (1) the impact of church history, (2) the impact of present polity, (3) the impact of pastoral tenure, and (4) the impact of current understanding. Each will list diagnostic questions to consider and a personal example from Mt. Zion Baptist Church, where I currently serve, and where I was first able to help lead a change in polity. Let's jump right into the first factor: the impact of church history.

FACTOR 1: THE IMPACT OF CHURCH HISTORY

One of the most important factors to consider when leading an organization to adopt a change in leadership structure is the organization's history.[1] A real-world example might be helpful here.

I know a brother who pastors a prominent and healthy church in the Southeastern United States. He has been there for several years and has brilliantly led the church through major staffing and facility issues. From all accounts, he has likely earned enough of

1. I know many feel this is "dwelling in the past," and we want to live in the here and now (or in the utopian future we have envisioned). I can already hear the objections of some: "This church's individual history doesn't negate the fact that Paul appointed multiple elders in all the churches he and Silas planted (Acts 14), that the church at Ephesus had multiple elders (Acts 20), or that Paul told Titus to appoint plural elders in every town (likely individual churches) in Crete. What is right is right, no matter what this church has experienced."

There is no doubt that Paul did those things; this pattern of leadership is evident throughout the New Testament, and I agree it is likely the best form of polity for every local church, regardless of its history. However, that does not negate the fact that the church's individual history will have a strong bearing on their response to this potential change.

the church's confidence to lead a change of this nature. *However*, when he first arrived, the church had recently dealt with a near split and lost many members, partly because the previous senior pastor tried to force a plural elder polity on the congregation. If my friend had ignored the church's history and decided to try to lead this change three or four years into his tenure, he likely would have experienced devastating consequences. Taking the church's history into account has helped steer him away from bad timing!

While your church may not have had such a dramatic event in its recent history, I would venture a guess that there are things that have taken place that—if you were aware of them—would have a significant bearing on the timing of leading a change in polity. That's because several factors about each church help identify its preparedness for a change like this and its potential reaction to it when introduced. Maybe they would cause you to accelerate the timing; maybe they would cause you to delay it; but they would have an impact. Let's examine some specific aspects to explore.

Consider the Church's Lifespan

In a one-hundred-twenty-year-old church, there are probably individuals who have been members for ten, twenty, thirty, forty, and even fifty-plus years. These members are like oak trees that have become deeply rooted and (likely) fixed in their ways. It is possible that they have seen the same model of leadership from their youth until now, making them more likely to adopt an "if it ain't broke, don't fix it" attitude to church leadership. In such a church, you will need to proceed much more slowly and cautiously.

Conversely, in a five-year-old church plant, the longest tenured member has been there for five years. These individuals are less vested in any particular leadership model. The current model isn't "the way their daddy and granddaddy did it." This form has not served them well for most of their life, and there is less nostalgia associated with the single pastor model. Additionally, in a newer—and hopefully growing—church plant, they have likely undergone more change recently—changes to facilities, staff, schedule, etc. Typically speaking, the more frequently someone deals with change, the more comfortable they become with it. In such a church, you will likely be able to introduce the idea earlier and move more quickly.

Identify the Church's Perspective on Change

When I perform funerals for senior saints, I often reflect on the numerous changes they have experienced during their years on earth. Many began their lives without indoor plumbing or telephones, but passed during an age with automatic toilets and smartphones!

Any organization that has existed for multiple decades has also had to embrace changes; this is the nature of the world. If your church has been around for five years, they have had to embrace multiple changes (think about COVID), and if it has been around for fifty years, it has had to navigate even more.

This is valuable to leaders considering introducing a major change in an organization, because organizations establish patterns and identities much like people do. I can look at an individual's office or living room and see how often they rearrange things and understand a good bit about how they embrace change. Some people drive the same car until the wheels fall off, not because they are cheap, but simply because they don't like change. While others trade in cars every three years, simply to get something new and different. These patterns reveal a person's perspective on change.

Likewise, researching how the church has reacted to its numerous changes can provide insight into what to expect when introducing another change. Look back over the church's history to identify its attitude toward change. If it has handled it well—or even sought out change—then you can likely move more quickly into considering a change in polity. However, if they have had the same carpet for the past seventy-five years, then you will probably need to slow way down.

PERSONAL EXPERIENCE

As I began to consider the history of Mt. Zion Baptist Church (MZBC), there were several things that immediately caught my attention. For starters, the church was almost two hundred years old and had maintained the same single pastor polity for longer than any current member had been alive. That told me that this leadership structure was deeply ingrained in the hearts and minds of the congregation, and that extensive groundwork would need to be laid before beginning any formal conversations about changing the polity. There were many members who saw this polity as being deeply personal as well.

I can vividly remember sitting in a deacon meeting and hearing one brother ask, "Now, Brother Zach, you are making it sound like this thing you are proposing is the right way to do things, but the way we currently do it is how my daddy and granddaddy did it. Are you telling me they were wrong?" I explained to him that this was not necessarily a right vs. wrong issue but an opportunity to take something that was already healthy and make it even healthier. I used the analogy of someone who exercises regularly and is in pretty good shape, but whose doctor then recommends they begin eating more vegetables. The doctor wasn't saying they were unhealthy, but instead was offering an avenue by which they could become even healthier. This explanation was well received, but in that moment, I learned a lesson I have shared in this chapter: A long-established and deeply ingrained polity is likely a very personal polity to the members of the church!

As I researched, I realized MZBC had established this polity well before anyone currently living was born, so there were no personal ties to the original architect of it, which was helpful information.

The last bit of information I gathered from the church's history was encouraging in many ways: MZBC had a recent history of embracing change well. They had made the transition to adding contemporary music well before many Southern Baptist churches, had seamlessly added multimedia into the worship services, and were a one-hundred-ninety-seven-year-old church that happily met in a metal building with chairs instead of pews and stained concrete floors. The church had shown a healthy willingness to embrace changes it felt would be in the long-term interest of the church and good for the kingdom.

Obviously, the church's history offered a bit of a mixed bag. There were some factors (lifespan of both the church and the current polity) that said we needed to approach the topic very slowly, but there were other factors (personal ties to the architect of the polity and willingness to change) that indicated that we would likely be able to proceed a bit more quickly once the idea was fully introduced.

These factors, along with those listed below, began to paint a clear picture of where our starting place needed to be, and what our moving pace could be once we started the formal process of changing the polity.

Diagnostic Questions

Here are a few questions to help you evaluate the church's perspective on change and its bearing on your starting place and moving pace.

- How did the church manage the transition from singing exclusively out of the hymnal to adding contemporary songs?
- How did they handle the introduction of new A/V equipment, such as TVs or projectors?

- How well did the church endure the changes of the 2020 pandemic?
- If they have ever had to relocate or undergo a major building project, how did that impact the church?
- If the church has become more racially diverse, how did they navigate that change?
- Has the church introduced live streaming services, multiple services, new staff positions, or seen a long-tenured pastor retire? If so, how well did they navigate these changes?

Here are a couple of hypothetical scenarios and what they could tell you about the church's readiness to begin this change.

These are examples of major concerns about readiness: if the church fired the music minister who first tried to sing "These are the Days of Elijah," or introduced an acoustic guitar; if the pastor who recommended the church consider starting a Facebook page found himself fine-tuning his resume; if the first guests with a different skin color were banned from entering the sanctuary; if the church exhibits patterns similar to these, you may want to reconsider your aspirations for leading a change in polity over the next few months. You will likely need years to get them ready.

Some examples of mild concerns about readiness include the following: the church navigated the pandemic without major issues, but it did have concerns about online giving. The church still has some members who complain about the instruments used on Sunday morning, but most are accepting of them. The _______ Sunday school class grumbled internally for a month about having to move rooms but didn't cause a real stir or any disunity. If the church exhibits similar patterns, you are probably in a position to begin considering the change while moving slowly towards it over the next year.

The church is ready if the church excitedly embraced adding screens and technology to the worship service; if they changed the weekly schedule to accommodate growth without issue; if they have added and removed new staff positions with ease; if they have changed locations or buildings without any hiccups. If the church exhibits similar patterns, then it may be ready to begin this change in as soon as a few months.

FACTOR 2: THE IMPACT OF PRESENT POLITY

The church's current polity carries a history with it as well. Everything that exists has a beginning, and the beginning of the church's current leadership structure can have a much heavier impact than you might expect. Consider the following aspects of the church's present polity and the impact they could have on the timing and pace of such a change.

The Polity's Lifespan

If you are pastoring a long-established church, you need to find out when they began implementing the present polity. If they have had the same polity for decades, you will likely encounter significant opposition when trying to change it. The church likely hired you with the expectation that you would integrate into their current system, not come in and change it.

If the church is a long-established, traditional Southern Baptist church, it has likely utilized a polity that mirrors the bicameral system of the US Congress for many years.[2] Although this model seems to deviate significantly from what we find in the New Testament, it is the one that the church has become very familiar with. In that case, it is essential to recognize that this system is not only the way they currently function but is possibly part of their identity. Many churches consider this model to be the "traditional Southern Baptist model." To ask them to consider an elder polity can seem more Presbyterian than they are comfortable with. Recognizing how tightly the present polity is tied to the church's

2. In this traditional system, the single pastor and deacon body function like the House of Representatives and the Senate, each wielding much local authority, including the authority to override a decision made by the other.

identity is critical when deciding how far you are from introducing a new polity.

Another critical point is that churches can often consider their present polity as being deeply personal. How could that be? For just a moment, stop to think about polity from their perspective. Their parents, grandparents, and possibly even great-grandparents were part of this system. Men whom they love and admire have served as deacons and pastors in this structure, and they have invested a lot of time and effort into this system. That means anything you say or do that is considered an "attack" on the structure could very well feel like a personal attack on the members and their families.

Just because a church has maintained its polity for a long time does not mean that all hope of leading a change is lost; it simply means that you will need to do more groundwork before beginning the process of changing the polity, and you will likely need to move more slowly once you do.

Diagnostic Questions

Here are a few questions to help you evaluate the polity and its impact on your starting place and moving pace.

- How long has the church had its present polity in place?
- How many members have personal ties to this structure (family members who have served as pastors or deacons)?
- How well has this polity served the church?
- Is the present polity a point of pride for the church?
- Is the present polity recognized as part of the church's identity?

If the church has had its current polity in place for decades, then you will likely need to build many years of trust before seeking to lead a change. If this polity seems to have served the body well, if they take pride in it or anchor their identity in it, then you likely need to add another year or two to that number.

The issue with personal ties doesn't have as much to do with finding your starting place but more to do with your moving pace. If the members have deep personal ties to the polity (parents or grandparents who served as pastors or deacons), then you will simply need to move more slowly and to regularly clarify that you are not calling the old structure wrong but simply offering one that could enhance the church's health.

The Polity's Architect

Some of you really love your dogs. Some because "He's a really good dog," and others because, like the previous section, you have had him for a long time. However, there is another reason why someone might deeply love their dog: because of who gave them the dog.

Some churches love their polity not because it is a necessarily great polity, or because of the amount of time it has been in place, but because of its architect. Perhaps the present polity was introduced by a pastor who served the church for twenty-five years, or maybe it was the church planter who founded the church. In either scenario, the church can feel a strong affection for the polity because of its architect.

Again, in this scenario, you find a church that has strong ties to its current polity. They view it as being precious and valuable to them. When attempting to lead such a church to change its polity, you will again need to move slowly and cautiously. However, if the current polity was implemented by a pastor who stayed for two years or who did not serve with distinction, then the body probably has less affinity for the model.

It is easy to think of the present polity as nothing more than an obstacle in your way to getting the church to where you want it to be. However, when properly examined, the present polity can be a useful tool to help determine the proper starting place and moving pace!

Diagnostic Questions

Here are a few questions that can help you evaluate the polity and its bearing on your starting place and moving pace.

- Who was the architect of the present polity?
- What was the architect's tenure like?
- Why was this polity put in place?

If the church has a polity established by a deeply beloved pastor or leader, you will likely need to serve for several years before considering a change to the polity. You will need to stay long enough to establish yourself as a faithful pastor who cares deeply about the church as well.

FACTOR 3: EVALUATING PASTORAL TENURE

In his book *They Smell Like Sheep*, Lynn Anderson says, "Trust is earned, not demanded, and it is built over time."[3] He also goes on to say, "Being placed in a leadership position does not guarantee a following, but a trail of sheep will usually follow the voice of a trusted shepherd."[4] These quotes reflect a truth that most pastors come to realize: you don't receive the complete, unadulterated trust of a congregation the day you step into the office; you must earn it over time.

In this section, we will evaluate factors like time that help build trust. In each subsection, we will consider quantifiable factors that will help you identify the proper starting place and moving pace for leading this change in your current context.

Length of Your Tenure

One of the most critical factors impacting a congregation's trust in a leader is time. Specifically, how long he has served in that local

3. Anderson, *They Smell Like Sheep*, 25.
4. Anderson, *They Smell Like Sheep*, 26.

church. There is a common saying among pastors: "It takes five years for the church to consider you their pastor." This is obviously an estimate, but it is based on the extensive experience of many seasoned pastors. You may receive the title and expectations of senior pastor on day one, but earning trust takes much longer.

During a few years of faithful service, you have invested a lot of time and effort into leading the church, praying for members, learning their names, visiting with and teaching them. However, consider things from their perspective. They have only seen you a couple of days a week and still haven't had the chance to get to know you well. Getting to know someone takes time, and time takes, well, time! This process cannot be sped up.

If the members are still getting to know you, then you need to wait longer before undertaking the campaign to change the church's polity. That doesn't mean you can't begin having conversations and laying groundwork, but that's probably as far as you need to go. Show patience and wait until you have earned their trust.

Diagnostic Questions

Here are some diagnostic questions that can help you consider whether you have gained the congregation's trust.

- Do members regularly come to you seeking personal or pastoral advice?
- Do the members often ask you to preach at funerals or officiate weddings, or do they still ask the previous pastor to come back?
- In committee meetings, do the members often want your feedback on potential plans?
- Do the members include you in family traditions like reunions or retirement parties?
- In moments of crisis, are you one of the first calls that members make?

If several of these characteristics of confidence are present and have been for a long time, then you are likely ready to lead a change in polity. If you are beginning to see a few of them, but there are still several that are lacking, or if they are exhibited by a few families but not most, then you are likely getting closer. However, if you don't see these characteristics, then be patient and put in the necessary time to help the body see you as their pastor before considering a change like this.

Average Length of Pastoral Tenures

The first church I ever served as a full-time staff member was Bethel Baptist Church in Monticello, Mississippi. I was in my early twenties, and after three years, it felt like I had been forever (it was over 10 percent of my life). However, that church was known for having long-tenured staff members. They had a string of senior pastors who stayed fifteen-plus years, and the church has had three music ministers over the last four decades! To them, my three years seemed like a drop in the bucket; we were just warming up.

Other churches run through a pastor every three years. In a church like that, staying for two to three years can seem like a significant investment, and remaining in place for four to five years can seem like an unexpected blessing! In such a church, you are likely to gain relational capital and the congregation's trust much more quickly.

Consider the average tenure of pastors at the church. Review the minutes, consult with the local association director, or discuss it with some members. Knowing the average tenure can help you understand how they likely view your time investment.

Diagnostic Questions

- What is the average tenure of pastors over the entire history of the church?

- What is the average tenure of pastors over the previous twenty-five years?
- What is the average tenure of the last three pastors?

This one is pretty simple. If you have served there longer than the previous few pastors, then you are likely ready to begin leading a change in polity. If your tenure is close to matching theirs, you might consider leading a change like this, but it may require a bit more time. If you are far shy of the average tenure of the last few pastors, then you need to be patient and wait until you gain more trust.

Opportunities to Lead

Years ago, my wife and I went to buy a house. We were young, had paid for everything with cash, and didn't have a credit card. The banker said, "I'm sorry, but you have no credit history." This didn't make sense to me. How could someone who never missed a single payment have a bad credit score? The banker quickly clarified: "I'm not saying you have a bad credit score, but you simply have no credit history at all."

Before undertaking an endeavor of this magnitude, you need to ask yourself, "Do I have any leadership history at this church?" If all you have done there is preach, lead some Bible studies, and meet with committees, you may be doing what is needed of you, but not enough to have earned the leadership capital needed to lead a change in polity.[5]

The church has not seen you in a leadership role. They have not seen you casting vision or experienced your ability to inspire and motivate individuals to buy into a new plan. Therefore, they are unlikely to be confident in your ability to lead them through such a major change as this.

5. I want to be very careful here. To say "all you have done is" sounds demeaning. I do not mean it that way at all. This is faithful shepherding, and it is valuable to the body and the kingdom. It is the work the Lord calls us to. The phrase "all you have done" is used only in the context of leading major change. While these things are faithful and valuable, they are not typically considered "organizational leadership."

Diagnostic Questions

- Have you led any changes in scheduling?
- Have you introduced a new annual event?
- Have you led the church to adopt a new mission partner?
- Have you led the church to hire a new staff member or restructure the current staff roles?
- Have you led a capital campaign for a new building, renovation, or debt retirement?

If the church has seen you lead several of these changes, then they probably have a good feel for your ability and style of leadership. If they have not, then you likely need to wait until you have had the opportunity to lead some of these changes before moving to something as significant as the church's polity. Something that is likely even more important than having had the opportunity to lead is how well you have led. Let's consider that for a moment.

Ability to Lead

If you have no credit history, you can build it fairly quickly. However, if you have a bad credit history, then trying to repair it is expensive and extensive.

Similarly, if you have no leadership history, you can gain some by leading smaller projects. However, if you have led projects that went sour or initiated processes that fell apart before completion, it is very hard to regain the trust of the body. If this is you, then the body will likely be very apprehensive about following you on something as large as a change in polity. Like credit history, leadership history follows you.

Diagnostic Questions

- Did you lead the church through the pandemic? If so, how effectively did you lead?

- If the church has experienced major conflict during your tenure, did you help resolve it in a healthy manner?
- If you have led a building campaign, how did the project turn out? Did it get completed by the projected deadline? Was the debt more significant and crippling than expected?
- If you have led the church to create strategic relationships with mission entities or other groups, have those relationships proved fruitful?

This type of assessment is often difficult and requires an outside opinion. Be willing to ask others to help you make this honest assessment. If you have led through great difficulty on multiple occasions, and the issues have been resolved neatly and in a timely manner, then the church will likely trust you to lead this change. If they have seen you lead and the results have been mixed, then you may need to give yourself some more time before beginning this change. However, if you have led poorly, then you will likely need a considerable amount of time (likely years) to regain the trust of the congregation.

PERSONAL EXPERIENCE

I was shocked to discover that the longest-tenured pastors in MZBC history had served for just ten years! There were two men who had both served for about ten years, but in the almost two-hundred-year history of the church, no one had stayed longer than a decade. In fact, going back to the 1960s, the average tenure of a pastor at MZBC was just over four years. This suggested that serving the church for five years or more would likely earn more trust than it would in many other churches. Five years or more would seem like a significant investment to the church.

I began serving MZBC in 2017, and am still currently serving here. Yes, that means I was here through the COVID-19 pandemic. Yes, I had the privilege of helping guide the church through governmental regulations and suggestions that had not been seen in nearly one hundred years. We had many senior adult members who were deeply scared of the virus, and therefore, of meeting with others in person. We also had many young families who felt the entire thing was a hoax. We had to add online giving, work through social distancing, and consider all the other challenges churches faced in those days.

However, one thing we were able to do was to begin a weekly drive-in parking lot service. We had a facility tailor-made for that purpose, and we quickly put this plan into place. While most churches were watching videos on Facebook or YouTube, we were able to gather together, albeit outside, each and every week. This allowed Mt. Zion to stay connected to one another in a way that people deeply missed during that season.

We gained members, saw steady giving, and appeased both those who felt we should gather weekly and those who were genuinely scared by the news. There were other, smaller opportunities I had to lead in those first few years as well. We made necessary revisions to our bylaws, changed our weekly schedule, and reformatted the way we tested and trained deacons. By the grace of God, all of these went well, and I felt I had some inherent trust from the church because of it.

After considering the church's history with pastoral tenure and recognizing how they viewed mine, both in terms of a time investment and in trusting my leadership, I was much more confident about the opportunity to lead this change. These indicators suggested they had a healthy level of trust in my ability to lead such a change, which gave me the confidence to begin the process.

LEVEL OF UNDERSTANDING

If you go to the doctor and he says you have a terrible blockage in one of your main arteries and need to cut out all fried foods, you will likely do it. That's because you have heard of heart disease and understand fried foods can contribute to it. However, if your doctor told you to cut out all fried foods because you have G9 bovine hoof disease, you will likely be skeptical and want more information. That's because we generally like making informed decisions.

This desire highlights another critical factor that needs to be considered: the level of familiarity the members and leaders have with this model of church leadership. If the leaders and members have never seen it or heard of it, they are likely to meet the idea with apprehension and skepticism, much like you would with your doctor. However, if many of them have a basic understanding of this model and have seen other churches that are led by a plural elder polity, then they are more likely to embrace the idea.

Diagnostic Questions

Here are some diagnostic questions to help you identify how familiar the church is with this polity.

- Are the staff or leaders familiar with this concept from seminary?
- Has this polity ever been taught or discussed at the church?
- If it has been introduced, how was it received?
- Does the church have any previous members serving another church with this polity?[6]
- Are there any previous staff who have gone on to serve churches with this polity?

6. It is possible that some young men or women who grew up in your church have gone on to serve as pastors, deacons, teachers, or members of churches or church plants that have a plural elder polity. If this is the case, you can expect a few families to be familiar with the concept.

- Does the church have any closely aligned sister churches with this polity?[7]

What you are looking for here is not necessarily expertise but familiarity. Is there a segment of the body that is at least familiar with the concept, or is it completely new to everyone?

If several staff members and leaders are very familiar with this concept and have openly discussed it with members and classes, you are in a strong position to begin leading this change soon. If the church has a degree of familiarity from sister churches or former members, then you are on the right track, but you will need some more time. However, if the concept is completely new, then you will need to lay extensive groundwork and will need to proceed very slowly once the idea is introduced.

PERSONAL EXPERIENCE

At Mt. Zion, I was fortunate to discover that there were several levels of familiarity with a plural elder polity, to such an extent that I would categorize it as unusual and unexpected. There were no other staff members serving when I arrived, but several lay leaders and deacons were familiar with the concept because a previous pastor had already introduced the concept. Although he didn't teach it to the membership as a whole, he had enough of these personal conversations that, when I arrived, several men and women in key leadership positions were already convinced that we needed to make this transition.

Another unique discovery was that MZBC had several families with sons serving as elders in churches that employ this polity. Three young men from MZBC accompanied Tony Merida to North Carolina to help plant Imago Dei Church and continued to serve there. Two others helped plant Immanuel NOLA in New Orleans and served there. That means there was

7. Think about churches in the same association or state convention.

already some familiarity built into the fabric of the membership; this was not a brand-new idea to them.

These factors all contributed to MZBC's ability to make this transition sooner and more smoothly than we might have otherwise. Knowing there was backing from the staff and familiarity among the body helped me see the amount of groundwork that had already been done, work I didn't have to do. Once I began exploring this idea more fully, these indicators gave me great confidence in our ability to move more quickly than average.

CONCLUDING THOUGHTS

In real estate, they say there are three significant factors to be understood and exploited: location, location, and location. Obviously, there are other factors, but none is more important than location! When it comes to leading a transition in polity, I am convinced that—outside of the grace and guidance of God—there are no more critical factors than timing, timing, and timing!

There may never be a moment that feels like the "perfect time," but I can guarantee you there are many that are not perfect. Each of these imperfect times carries different hazards. When beginning too early, people will likely not trust you or lack the necessary understanding. In this scenario, the church will likely vote "no" on the change due to uncertainty. If you introduce the idea but wait too long to make a formal move to change, members may lose enthusiasm. In this scenario, you may eventually lead the transition, but it will lack the excitement and joy that could have been found earlier.

Another factor I consider, alongside the timing of beginning the process, is the pace at which you move through it. Things take time to digest. New concepts need an opportunity to marinate. You have to continually evaluate your timing. Are we introducing new concepts and aspects too quickly, too slowly, or just right? Keeping this in mind throughout the process will be a key factor in the success of the process.

The factors listed in this chapter are all important, and they all take time or research. Don't jump the gun. Take your time, do the hard work of laying the groundwork, and you will be thankful later. Asking questions, examining the church's history, and honestly assessing how the body views you will help you understand the change from their perspective. Once you see it the way they do, you can begin working with your leadership team to develop a realistic timeline for the transition. Perhaps it can begin now, or maybe in two to three years; possibly, you're looking at another five years or more.

PERSONAL PLEA

This chapter contains numerous leadership principles and diagnostic questions. Take time to work through each step before proceeding. The rest of this book is hyper-focused on leading the actual transition. It covers what to teach, when to teach it, how to discuss the concept, how to implement this polity, how to train men to serve in it, etc.

Perhaps you need to take a week to assess your readiness, and then return to the book. However, it is possible that some of you may need to take a couple of months or years to lay a solid foundation before moving forward.

I'm not literally asking you not to read the rest of the book until the time comes. However, I do want to exhort you to take the assessment phase seriously. Don't get too excited and simply jump into the process before the church is ready.

PERSONAL EXPERIENCE

When you hear all the things MZBC had going for it, you might think I jumped right in to leading this transition.

> We had members familiar with the concept, trusted and vested leaders clamoring for it, and the church had shown a propensity to joyfully embrace changes that would lead to greater health for the body.
>
> However, I was here for five years before I ever began formally discussing this transition. Let that sink in for a moment. I found myself with a better opportunity than likely 90 percent of pastors will, and I waited five full years before doing anything!
>
> Why did you wait so long, you might ask? There were several reasons, but the most pertinent were that I needed time to earn the church's trust, they needed time to understand who I am as a leader, and I wanted to work through these assessment questions and lay more groundwork before deciding to move forward.

After you consider these assessment questions and believe the church is ready to begin this process, it is time to get to work. The next phase will be the education phase. Let's consider how you can help the congregation to begin to see the need for multiple pastors/elders.

2

Displaying the Need

Helping the Congregation See Your Perspective

When I was in high school, I wanted to be a mechanic. I got an after-school job working at Danny Sharp's Auto Repair Shop. One day, I was changing the oil in a vehicle but could not remove the stubborn oil filter. I tried everything: my bare hand, a rag, an oil filter wrench, but all to no avail. The problem was that I simply wasn't strong enough to do it on my own; I ended up having to ask someone for help.

This was a particularly frustrating experience. Some of you have been in a similar boat before. You have had a job or assignment that you simply could not complete. Maybe you didn't have the time, the skills, the strength . . . but no matter the reason, not being able to complete it probably left you feeling frustrated or defeated. Just as I needed help with the oil filter, pastors often find that the work placed on them is too great for one man to handle. They need more hands than they have. This feeling is particularly prevalent for solo pastors.

You want to be there for every sick member, pray before every surgery, and preach at every funeral. You want to officiate weddings, lead services, direct ministries, care for your family, and attend every committee meeting.

However, we are bound by time and space. We cannot be in two places at once. Often, this requires us to decide between one important thing (being at a surgery, visiting a member) and another important thing (studying to preach, attending a counseling session or a committee meeting). None of these things are unimportant, so being forced to neglect some is very frustrating.

There are other limitations that also frustrate pastors. There is the frustration of wanting to be a perpetually available pastor while also wanting to be a good and present father and husband. There's the frustration of lacking ability: we aspire to be the best teacher, leader, counselor, and administrator so that the churches we serve will be blessed in every facet of pastoral leadership. We aspire to preach like Adrian Rogers, evangelize like Billy Graham, and lead like Spurgeon. We hope to counsel like Paul David Tripp, direct missions like William Carey, and write like C. S. Lewis. Yet, we must acknowledge that God has only gifted us in certain areas.

These frustrations should be part of what leads us to desire a plural elder polity. We *know* we don't possess all the gifts in their full capacity, so we desire to serve alongside men who possess different gifts. We know we can't attend every event, committee meeting, and home visit, so we desire to have more hands to share the load. We recognize the challenge of prioritizing among these tasks, and we aim to be part of a team that can address them all. However, most of our fellow members don't get it. This isn't necessarily their fault; they simply can't see things from our perspective.

What these members need is a shift in perspective. They need us to help them recognize the need in the same way we do. Let's consider ways we could do this.

HELPING CHURCH MEMBERS UNDERSTAND THE NEED FOR MORE ELDERS

You get it, you feel the frustrations deep down in your soul. You are hurt by having to abandon meaningful tasks and ignore others. You can see the vision of how a plurality of elders would make such a difference, and you wonder, "Why don't they get it?" You are baffled that the other church members don't share your concerns and desires? You wonder, "Why isn't this something they are clamoring for?"

Many church members don't desire a change in leadership structure because they don't know what a difference it would make. They have no idea how useful this would be.

In general, I find that people aren't opposed to being cared for more completely, being led by a more gifted team, or allowing their pastors to care for the church and his family more fully. They simply don't realize the need.

They don't realize how often you have to put one task on hold to complete another. They aren't sitting at home thinking about you attending a committee meeting during your son's little league game. They are unaware that you left your family vacation early to return for a funeral or wedding, as you are the only pastor the church has. They aren't sitting around and thinking about you or church leadership structures at all!

It's part of your job to help them see this need. Oftentimes, we misunderstand how difficult a job is until we have done it ourselves. This reminds me of the time I tried to build a kitchen table.

A few years ago, my seven-year-old son and I worked together to build a kitchen table. It was our first real carpentry project, and it took longer—and was harder—than expected. I realized that you need to understand various aspects, including types of wood, carpentry tools, geometry, stains, varnishes, and more. By the time we completed the ten-by-four-foot farm table, I had a deep appreciation for carpenters!

Just as I had no idea how difficult carpentry was until I tried my hand at it, most church members lack a clear understanding of what all pastoral ministry entails. Obviously, we can't simply let every member pastor for a few weeks to gain first-hand knowledge of the role, so the next best thing is to teach them the role. Take the time to explain what they should expect of their pastor. Don't teach them what *you* want them to expect, but teach them what the Bible says they should expect.

If you want your fellow members to understand why the church needs multiple pastors, you have to start by helping them understand the biblical role of pastors. Many are completely ignorant, leading to such demeaning jokes as, "I wish I were a pastor; they only work one day a week." Help them see there is much more to pastoring than the work that occurs in the pulpit on Sunday morning. Scripture lists many tasks, duties, and responsibilities given to pastors. Take time to walk through these and help the congregation understand what they look like in practice.

However, teaching the church the biblical role of a pastor is not the only thing you will need to do to help them understand the need for multiple elders. Actually, that is the easy part. After helping them understand the biblical role of an elder, you must also be vulnerable and help them recognize that you aren't fulfilling this role completely (none of us are). This requires you to be open about some of the struggles and concerns you have. Share specific examples of tasks you have had to leave undone in order to prioritize other duties. Help them understand that you desire that they have more pastoral guidance, mentoring, and care in their lives, but that you simply aren't capable of doing all these things fully. This will help them understand that this need is not just biblical but pastoral. You aren't simply trying to fill a job description but to care for their souls.

The following section will offer a detailed outline of how to go about this process. I will share the biblical texts I walked through at Mt. Zion to help flesh out the full role of pastoral leadership. I will then detail how I connected these biblical teachings with my pastoral heart. I believe that when these two things are done in conjunction, they create an atmosphere where members will begin to desire a more comprehensive polity.

TEACHING THE ROLE OF PASTOR/ELDER/ OVERSEER IN A NEW TESTAMENT CHURCH

Here are the sections of Scripture I used to teach Mt. Zion the biblical role of a pastor/elder (with a basic outline for each). These are not the only texts you can turn to, but I believe they offer a helpful overview for those who are unaware of the tasks given to the office.

Acts 20:17–35

In this text, Paul has one last face-to-face meeting with the Ephesian elders he personally trained and served alongside. In this meeting, he informs them of the expectations of their roles as pastors/elders. This list includes

- living exemplary lives (v. 18),
- teaching in public and in private, to large groups and to individuals (v. 20),[1]
- working as an evangelist to share the gospel with all (v. 21),
- teaching the whole counsel of God (v. 27),
- serving as a shepherd who knows and lives among the people he leads (v. 28–30),
- offering oversight to the church as a whole (v. 28),
- protecting against false teachers from outside of the church (v. 29–30), and
- leading in calling out false teachers within the church (v. 28–30).

I recommend beginning by simply teaching through this text. It can be done on a Sunday morning, Sunday night, Wednesday night, or in some special setting (i.e., Friday through Saturday seminar). Next, help the congregation visualize what each of these tasks looks like in real life. Give them examples of how you and other pastors you know do these things. Help them understand what the Bible says *and* what each one practically looks like.

Some of these areas are more familiar to the congregation than others. They understand that pastors teach, evangelize, and

1. These categories almost certainly encompass both preaching, teaching, and counseling.

preach. However, behind-the-scenes roles like protecting against false teachers and shepherding are often unseen.

To help them understand the importance of protecting against false teachings and teachers, I explained my consideration of the songs we sing and the materials used for small groups and Sunday school. I also highlighted that I individually encourage people to critically evaluate the content they consume.

The area I spent the most time fleshing out was "shepherding." I began by explaining that this is what the term "pastor" truly means, and we explored the ways pastoral ministry is similar to actual shepherding.

I emphasized the importance of spending time with members outside the church's walls—visiting, interacting at their workplaces, the fishing hole, or the ballpark. I also explained how I seek to attend birthday parties, weddings, funerals, retirement celebrations, and other significant events. I told them that I keep up with them through conversations in the community, reading the local paper, or social media.

As pastors, we know we do this to better understand them, to recognize their strengths and weaknesses, and to identify areas where they need exhortation or encouragement. We also do this so we can weep with them when they weep and rejoice with them when they rejoice.

This is much of what it means to be a shepherd, a pastor. A good shepherd knows his sheep individually, and a good pastor knows the members of the church personally.

It takes a lot of time and intentionality to shepherd well, and this is only one task given to pastors. Once the congregation understood this, it helped move the needle on their understanding of the expansiveness of the roles and responsibilities of this office.

Acts 20 is a great text for helping the body see the full breadth of pastoral ministry. However, a text that shows a more specific role, and the pivotal impact of that role, is found in Eph 4.

Ephesians 4:11–14

The call to "equip the saints for the work of ministry"[2] is a foundational calling for all pastors. At Mt. Zion, we considered this calling and its implications. First, we looked at the idea that pastors (and leaders) are not called to do all the ministerial work themselves, but this calling is given to all members. Second, we looked at what it means to "equip" someone.[3] I explained how pastors must serve as mentors and trainers for church members.

As with most things, I found a concrete illustration helpful here. We discussed the concept of an internship, with a particular emphasis on how Jesus prepared the apostles for their upcoming work.[4] I helped the church think about a pastor as one who is called to spend time with the members, walk with them, invite them to do ministry alongside him, help fill in knowledge and skill gaps they have, help them identify and hone their spiritual gifts, and eventually deploy them to overtake individual areas of ministry leadership. This pattern is clearly seen with Jesus and his disciples in Luke 9 and 10.

Helping them see the pastor as a mentor and trainer who is capable and committed to equipping members for ministry added another layer to their understanding of the role of pastoral leadership in a church. Pastors aren't simply the professionals hired to do all the work; they are skilled leaders preparing others to work alongside them.

Alongside this teaching, I emphasized the outcome of this role. If it is done well, then the members all become more spiritually mature, the "whole body, joined and held together by every joint with which it is equipped, when each part is working properly, makes the body grow so that it builds itself up in love."[5] Not

2. Eph 4:12.

3. Frank Thielman—in his commentary on Ephesians in the Baker series—is extremely helpful here. Thielman, *Ephesians*, 277–80.

4. One resource I found helpful here is the book *The Mentoring Church*. Newton, *Mentoring Church*, 29–32.

5. Eph 4:16.

only is mentoring a clear pastoral duty, it is one that—when neglected—has severe consequences for the body.

The final text we considered to help flesh out the tasks, duties, and responsibilities of pastoral leadership was 1 Tim 3:1–7.

1 Timothy 3:1–7

This is a section we typically turn to when considering ordaining a pastor, and most of the requirements listed are more about character than skill or ability. However, I believe some of these requirements also reflect the roles and responsibilities of pastors. By helping the congregation consider the ideas of being "able to teach," "manage his household well," and the trustworthiness required to remain "above reproach," I helped the members of Mt. Zion extend their thinking about the role of a pastor even further.

"Able to Teach"—1 Timothy 3:2

The first pastoral requirement I covered is the simplest to understand and the one you likely need to spend the least time on with your members—they know pastors should be able to teach. However, they don't necessarily understand what all teaching entails. Some people assume that attending seminary means you know everything and can simply stand up on Sunday mornings and deliver a sermon.

I helped the congregation consider the time required to teach effectively and revisited the various teaching areas outlined in Acts 20, which all pastors are expected to cover. Help them understand that this requirement encompasses a wide range of activities, including preaching, counseling, small group settings, lesson development, one-on-one instruction, and more. Don't neglect to point out that each of these settings is best handled with preparation that takes time.

"Manage His Household Well"—1 Timothy 3:4–5

The second pastoral requirement I covered was management. The idea of managing a household is not the same as leading a family. To manage a household in the first century meant overseeing your family and all the support staff that would have been part of the household. In his commentary on Timothy, Philip Towner says, "The stipulation here initially exceeds issues of parenting and husbanding to include management of slaves, property, business interests, and even maintenance of important relationships with benefactors/patrons or clients."[6] In the first century, managing a household was more akin to running a small business than simply tending to a family, and in 1 Tim 3:4, Paul said men should have shown themselves capable of doing this if they were going to pastor.

This does not mean that a man must have extensive business acumen to serve as a pastor, but it is a reminder that pastoring is much more than preaching. Pastoring encompasses oversight of ministries and committees, leading in wise stewardship, providing guidance on resource investment, ensuring all members are cared for and heard equally, planning for the future, and undertaking other administrative and leadership tasks. While pastors are called to fulfill all these roles, and most work diligently at them, the majority of them take place in closed-door settings. The average member doesn't see your leadership as the finance committee considers the annual budget, the direction you offer to the deacon ministry on how to care for homebound members, or the conversations you have between members in conflict. So, this teaching session will offer an opportunity to help them understand the administrative and managerial role of the pastor more fully.

"Above Reproach"—1 Timothy 3:2

The final pastoral requirement I covered was the overarching requirement of being "above reproach."[7] I am convinced this re-

6. Towner, *Letters to Timothy and Titus*, 254.

7. 1 Tim 3:2.

quirement includes all the ones listed in verses 2–7 and signifies a great commitment to ongoing personal growth and holiness. For a pastor to remain a pastor, he must remain above reproach. This is not a one-time condition that, after a pastor is ordained, can be allowed to lapse. No, pastors must remain above reproach for the entirety of their ministry. This requires a man to continually oversee his own soul while overseeing the souls of others. Pastors must maintain a character and reputation that allow them to be a trusted leader, and this takes time and intentionality. He can't lead the church if he can't lead his household, and he can't oversee others if he can't oversee himself.

This teaching series is a large task that takes a lot of time, I know. You will have to work through the text yourself, develop the sermons, and set aside a time to teach through them. At this point, you might be wondering if all this work will be worth it, but believe me, it will.

As the congregation grows in its understanding of the pastor's role, you will likely see a shift in their appreciation for you.[8] Several key leaders will likely start offering more encouragement or taking items off your plate. More than these short-term implications, there are valuable long-term ones as well.

The intended outcome of this teaching may not immediately make sense. You might be thinking to yourself, "I want to lead the church to change its polity, not teach about the role of a pastor/elder." I understand your concern, but I would like to take a moment to explain why this is necessary.

AFFECTING THE HEAD

If members don't understand the role of a pastor, or if they discount it too greatly, then they aren't likely to think they need more

8. If you are uncertain if they have really grasped the complete role of a pastor, you could use a trusted online AI program to help you create a diagnostic tool or test, or simply do it yourself. Afterward, ask a segment of the congregation to complete the test. This can help you gauge their understanding more fully.

than one of them! I've already mentioned the old joke that pastors "only work one day a week." Though this thought is often shared in a joking manner, I fear the underlying notion is more prevalent than we might think. I have had friends and people in my own family honestly ask me what a full-time pastor does all week.

If we want the congregation to recognize the extensive work of pastoral ministry, we must use God's word to unashamedly show them what God expects of his undershepherds. These teaching sessions offer the opportunity to do that. This is your opportunity to demonstrate that this role is a significant one, encompassing multiple aspects of life and ministry. It is not only time-consuming, but it is life-giving! Help them gain a deeper understanding of what pastoring truly means.

However, people rarely change simply because of head knowledge. Even if they gain a comprehensive understanding of what pastoral ministry entails, they still need help converting this understanding into a desire for change. This is where that personal vulnerability comes in.

AFFECTING THE HEART

At this point, you have taken the time to prepare this special teaching series, gathered the church, taught them through all these texts, helped them see the role of a pastor, and increased their knowledge about what God expects of pastoral leadership. However, for many of us, the hard part is what comes next, vulnerably sharing that you aren't meeting these expectations.

None of us likes admitting failure. It is hard and uncomfortable. It requires a large dose of humility, but in many cases, it leads to good things; this is one of those cases. I won't say that this is absolutely necessary for the process of leading a transition in polity, but I believe a personal plea for help allows the members to see that this need for more pastors is not just a theoretical thing but a practical need in their local context. It also allows them to understand that this is not just something that would be beneficial for them but also something that would be beneficial for you!

So, let me encourage you to share openly and honestly about this need. Help them see that you genuinely desire to meet all their pastoral needs but that you simply can't. Tell them you long to serve alongside other men who serve for their good and God's glory. I believe this act of humility will go a long way in helping them understand this need in both their heads and their hearts.

PERSONAL EXPERIENCE

At Mt. Zion, I recounted all the roles and responsibilities listed in this chapter (loving shepherds, able leaders, adequate teachers, gifted equippers, watchful guardians, skilled mentors, trusted overseers and managers, and humble servants), and it wasn't hard for me to convince them I could not do all this alone. They knew there was no way I could spend adequate time with two hundred-plus members. I couldn't get to know them all well, walk with them regularly, learn their strengths and struggles, equip them all for the work of ministry, counsel each of them, regularly pray for them by name, prepare to preach and teach, oversee all the committees and teams, lead in resource allocation, staff development, and the other various duties assigned to me.

Once this point was established, I was honest and vulnerable with them. I told them how weighty this was for me. I knew there were things God expected of the pastoral leadership of this church, and I knew I was failing to do several of those things. I discussed the challenge of regularly reviewing a list of important tasks and deciding which ones to prioritize and which to neglect. I pleaded with them to think about how difficult this is. I related this to the feeling of having multiple children who all have games or recitals simultaneously. You want to attend and support them all, but you have to choose one or the other. Something is going to be left out.

I then asked this question out loud to the congregation: Did God set me up to fail? Did God set up Tim and Chris to fail?[9]

I then answered my own question with a resounding no! But this answer raised another question: If all these expectations are biblical and right, but God didn't set me up to fail, then what is missing? The answer to that lies in the false assumption that one man is supposed to do all these things alone. I told them it's as if we had been looking at option A) these expectations are not biblical, or B) one pastor should be able to do all these things, but the actual answer was C) God expects all these things to be done, but by more than one man.

This is where I began to make the shift from discussing the roles and responsibilities of pastors to examining the design of pastoral leadership in New Testament churches. For the first time, I introduced them to the idea of plural elder polity, explaining that I was convinced God had given pastoral leadership a calling too big for one man to fulfill because he never expected one man to do it all.

After introducing this idea, I took the time to highlight how the churches in the New Testament fulfilled this calling by having multiple men serve as pastors in each individual church.[10] This was a pivotal change that helped

9. Tim and Chris were previous pastors of Mt. Zion, men dearly loved by the congregation.

10. For more information, see any of these texts: Acts 14, 20; Titus 1; 1 Pet 5:1. I will not belabor this point because it is one most of you are well versed in and chomping at the bit to teach anyway! However, if you need additional resources about this pattern, let me offer a few books:

- *Elders in the Life of the Church: Rediscovering the Biblical Model for Church Leadership* by Phil Newton and Matt Schmucker. In my opinion, this book is the gold standard for introducing and understanding this subject.
- *Biblical Eldership: An Urgent Call to Restore Biblical Church Leadership* by Alexander Strauch. Strauch and I disagree on the authority given to elders (ruling elders vs. leading elders), but other than that, we see eye to eye on

> them see this was not just a bright idea I had come up with but one rooted in the pages of Scripture. This was momentous for helping them move forward in the transition process.

The task of helping the congregation see the need for a new leadership model is crucial to this process. It will take considerable time and effort, and it will require personal vulnerability. However, it is worth it! Before moving on, let's review what we have discussed in this chapter and why it is important.

CONCLUDING THOUGHTS

My wife and I have five children. They currently range from three to twelve years old, and when it comes time for Christmas or a birthday, there are always construction projects! Many of you know what I'm talking about: a bike, a playhouse, a set of bunk beds . . .

One time, my daughter wanted a dollhouse. I'm not talking about a dainty toy. No, it was a three-story, four-foot-tall monster with about a thousand pieces! The instructions said, "Assembly requires two individuals," but I didn't think that was necessary . . . until I got about halfway through the project and started yelling for help! Some jobs clearly need more than one person.

---

almost everything pertaining to this subject. Even with that one distinction, I can't recommend this book highly enough.

- *40 Questions About Elders and Deacons* by Benjamin Merkle. This is one of the most valuable books for you to read and put in the hands of church members. I bought multiple copies and offered them as a resource for members to check out and take home.
- *Church Elders: How to Shepherd God's People Like Jesus* by Jeremy Rinne. This is a short and accessible book that you can read in a day or two to get a solid introduction to the subject.

I'm convinced pastoral ministry is one of those jobs! I'm also convinced that it is part of your job to help the congregation see all that pastoral leadership actually entails. They don't currently understand it. They believe their current system is sufficient; however, they are unaware of what they are missing or the extent to which this affects you. Once they understand the vastness of the role, most of them will agree that it is too big for any one man to fulfill.

That is why I believe it is so valuable to start here. Help them see what they are missing out on, and work to show them your perspective. Give them a biblical understanding of all God expects of pastoral leadership, and then you will be ready to help them see a vision of what having multiple pastors could be like!

3

Feeling the Need

Helping the Congregation Desire the Change

THAT WAS IT; I knew I had to have one! The batteries in our golf cart were dead and needed replacement. I have a friend who recently installed a lithium-ion battery in his golf cart; he explained the benefits to me, and I could already picture it in my mind: my kids would be able to ride for longer, the golf cart would be lighter and faster, and I would save money in the long run. I was sold!

This instance of hearing about a product, being able to picture the difference it would make in your life, and deciding to purchase it is not an isolated event. This is one reason infomercials—as cheesy and annoying as they seem—work. When you watch one, you aren't only *hearing* about the product but are *seeing* the difference it would make in your life; this is invaluable!

When a company allows people to see *and* feel the difference a product would make, the people's understanding of the product can easily become a desire to have it. This is the next step in leading a change in polity: helping the congregation see and feel the difference this change would make in their lives.[1]

1. You are not a company or marketing agent and do not have a product to sell. You are a pastor or leader with something that could significantly enhance

In this chapter, I will list seven key benefits offered by a plural elder polity.[2] These benefits—clarified Christology, comprehensive coverage, greater giftedness, additional accountability, panoramic pastoring, distinct deacons, and stronger succession—are all meant to help the congregation understand and feel how beneficial this new polity would be.

For each benefit, I will outline the benefit, explain its purpose in teaching the congregation, provide teaching points to cover, and illustrate how it was implemented at MZBC.

SEVEN BENEFITS OF A PLURAL ELDER POLITY

Benefit 1: Clarified Christology

Aim: The congregation will see that adding more elders clarifies Jesus as the only Head of the church.

In many churches, if you polled one hundred members and asked, "Who is the head of this church?" the answer would likely be "Pastor ________."

I would argue that this view is particularly prevalent in a single elder polity because the optics seem to reflect reality. This one man appears to answer to no one; he seems to have complete autonomy, calls the shots, and everyone follows. It shouldn't be surprising, then, that in such a model, members can easily become confused and think of this man as the head of the church.

However, the apostle Paul paints a very different picture in Col 1:18. In this verse, Paul tells us that Jesus "is the head of the body, the church. He is the beginning, the firstborn from the dead, that in everything he might be preeminent." Theologically, none of us is arguing against this point, and none of our members would either. However, I am a firm believer that local application should reflect biblical actuality. What do I mean by that?

---

the spiritual lives of many people. However, when approached ethically, this principle is still very applicable.

2. These are not the only benefits offered by this transition but seven that seem particularly meaningful to pastors and members.

If Jesus is the sole Head of the church, then I believe every member (including the senior pastor) should display a level of humility, accountability, and submission, not only to God but also to other Christians.[3] I am convinced that this is not only spiritually healthy but also locally beneficial, as it allows the church to see a concrete reflection of the spiritual truth that the only autonomous and sovereign one is Christ.[4] When members see their senior pastor submitting not only to Scripture but to other Christians, when they hear him say that a new campaign or idea belongs to another brother, or when they see him sitting in the pew while another pastor is preaching, I believe it helps them understand that this man is not the head of the church. This is a benefit afforded by a plural elder polity.

So, take the time to help the church understand how this particular benefit would positively impact the body. Explain how their children and grandchildren, new members that come, and those who are confused about the head of the church can be helped to have a higher Christology by moving to a plural elder polity, one where every member of the church openly and regularly submits to others in recognition that Christ is the only sovereign and autonomous one.

PERSONAL EXPERIENCE

For the first six years I served at MZBC, *nothing* got done without it coming across my desk. I believe this is because the members genuinely believed I was the head of the church and that my approval was necessary for every task. This was not healthy for me or the church.

However, from the time we adopted a plural elder polity until now, there has been a noticeable change. There

3. Ephesians 5:21 calls for Christians to "submit to one another out of reverence for Christ." While this command is not specifically written to elders, it is written to all Christians, and elders are Christians.

4. For more thoughts on the importance of pastors/elders submitting to one another, see Wiesner, "Why Pastors Should Submit."

> are times when things have gotten done, and I wasn't the point person. I'm not talking about simple tasks; of course, there have always been new flower arrangements in the sanctuary, Sunday school materials ordered, and the grass was cut without anyone asking me. However, I'm talking about things more significant than that.
>
> Since we shifted our polity, there have been instances when quarterly reviews were handled by our personnel committee or our building and grounds undertook projects—with pastoral approval—that I was not directly involved in![5]
>
> I believe the shift to a plural elder polity has allowed MZBC to more fully understand that I am not the head of the church; Christ is, and that is good, healthy, and right!

Understanding that Jesus is the only Head of the church is a benefit that many theologically astute members will desire. It feels like one geared more toward leadership, but the second benefit is one that should resonate well with all members, as it explains how this transition will allow for greater coverage of pastoral duties.

Benefit 2: Comprehensive Coverage

Aim: The congregation will see that adding more elders will allow the workload of pastoral ministry to be divided more appropriately and covered more fully.

Have you ever heard the old adage "many hands make light work"? If you are a pastor, you have probably said this when trying to get members to come to a work day, and if you are a parent, you likely say it when trying to get your children to help clean up the house.

5. Each of our elders is responsible for overseeing at least one committee. They meet with them, offer pastoral insight where needed, and bring major concerns or questions to the rest of us at our next scheduled elders meeting.

There's a reason such adages have endured for hundreds of years and are frequently quoted by many of us—because they usually contain a great deal of truth. I won't insult your intelligence by explaining why this adage is true, but I do believe it is important to help your fellow members think about its application in pastoral ministry. From my experience, I am convinced this is one of the most practical benefits of transitioning to a plural elder polity, and one that the church can easily picture.

The majority of chapter 2 was spent laying out the argument that pastoring is not a one-man job. The tasks are too many (as we saw in Acts 20), and the implications too significant (Eph 4). Benjamin Merkle explains it this way in his book *40 Questions About Elders and Deacons*: "Caring for the church is often too much for one man to handle and can lead to frustration and burnout."[6]

However, when we have multiple elders serving in a single congregation, these tasks don't all fall on the shoulders of one man. This is beneficial because our shoulders are only so large, and when we try to do this alone, many of the things that fall on our shoulders end up falling to the wayside! Merkle goes on to say this later in the same paragraph, "A third benefit of having a plurality of elders is that the burden of the ministry is shared by others."[7]

When you have other pastors, you can divide the tasks and assignments. This allows all of them to be completed by called and qualified pastors without you having to do them all.[8] Imagine yourself as the sole pastor of a church on a week where there is a funeral to preach, premarital counseling to conduct, a committee meeting on Tuesday evening, and a new couple who wants to meet and discuss joining the church. All of that, and you still need

6. Merkle, *40 Questions*, 55.

7. Merkle, *40 Questions*, 185.

8. Some of you will ask about deacons at this point. You might be wondering why this workload can't simply be shared between a single pastor and deacons. This will be more fully addressed later in this chapter, but the short answer is that there are some tasks and responsibilities given to pastors alone. If these are handled by deacons, they are not being handled appropriately, and therefore should only be undertaken by ordained pastor/elders.

to be prepared for the midweek service, and of course, Sunday is coming!

In the above scenario, which tasks are worth simply putting off? Maybe you can reschedule the premarital counseling. It is possible to tell the couple wanting to join the church that you can't meet this week, and they'll have to wait. However, none of us wants to give the impression that these individuals aren't important. You're going to preach at the funeral and preach or teach on Wednesday and Sunday. So, you likely fit all these things in, but you probably end up neglecting your family, exceeding your limit, and possibly not preparing well for Wednesday or Sunday.

Now, imagine the same scenario in a plural elder polity. One pastor could handle premarital counseling, another could meet with the couple about membership, and a different pastor could cover Wednesday night services, allowing you to focus on caring for the family who has lost a loved one and preparing to preach on Sunday. In this scenario, you don't get burned out, your family doesn't get neglected, the couples aren't put off and made to feel unimportant, and all the pastoral duties are handled by qualified—and recognized—elders!

This is what pastoring with a team approach can look like. It is good for the body; it ensures that God's expectations of pastoral leadership are carried out without neglect, and it allows pastoral ministry to be more sustainable and enjoyable! However, if members never have this need explained to them, they might simply miss it. So, take the time to help them see the current need for more hands and how it could easily be provided by shifting to a plural elder polity.

PERSONAL EXPERIENCE

Just this week, I had a staff meeting on Monday morning, met with another pastor who needed guidance on Monday afternoon, was invited to speak alongside a mission team from our local church at an associational

> event, and will help serve at—and oversee—our church's food pantry ministry.
>
> I'm also scheduled to have a meeting with an IMB mission partner on Wednesday morning, a committee meeting on Wednesday afternoon, to teach twice on Wednesday, preach on Sunday, and give guidance and leadership to our staff. Oh, by the way, my son has his final ball games of the season, and we have a family Mother's Day cookout scheduled. In a single elder model, something would fall to the wayside, and none of these things can be kicked to next week!
>
> Thankfully, I'm not the only elder at our church. Therefore, I was able to ask two of our other elders to take on a few of these tasks, allowing them to be completed well, and I can still enjoy my wife, my mom, our son's final games, and serving as a pastor.
>
> At times, I will point out these things to the congregation, highlighting how our plurality has led to more tasks being completed with greater focus, intentionality, and timeliness. I don't just make this statement in general terms; I offer clear examples. Not only that, but the church can feel the difference. They know more pastoral tasks are being completed, they see the guidance they are being offered by called and qualified elders, they recognize there is a greater focus on each aspect of our public ministry (they can tell when you have taken adequate time to prepare to teach, preach, and present), and they appreciate these things.

This very practical and relatable benefit is an important one for the congregation to hear and see. A very similar benefit, with a slightly more theological underpinning, is that having more pastors also leads to an increase in spiritual gifting among the pastors.

Benefit 3: Greater Giftedness

Aim: The congregation will see that adding more elders will increase the spiritual giftedness of the eldership.

I absolutely love running. To lace up my shoes, put on my headphones, and go for a good six or seven-mile run is a perfect morning for me. I know that sounds absolutely ridiculous to many of you. You either can't run or can't stand to run. You can think of a million other things you would want to do on a day off.

Your thoughts effectively illustrate the point I want to make here: there are some things that you love doing and excel at that others can't do or don't want to do. Likewise, there are things others love doing and excel at that you simply can't. This is not only true physically but also spiritually.

There are multiple places in the New Testament where we find lists of spiritual gifts.[9] In these lists and Paul's teaching about the gifts in Eph 4, we learn that God has given each of us a different set of gifts.[10] Some are great teachers, some are gifted administrators, some are gifted in service, some in exhortation, some in giving, and some in mercy. . . . While all believers have at least one spiritual gift, Paul's teaching about our interdependence on one another[11] helps us recognize that none of us—not even pastors—possess the full complement of gifts.

Help the church understand how beneficial it is to have multiple men serving as pastors, as this plurality leads to a greater complement of giftings.

In a single elder model, the church only experiences the joy of being led by a few of these gifts. The church has one pastor; therefore, pastorally speaking, it can only benefit from the spiritual gifts he has, nothing more. The church misses out on being led by all the gifts he lacks. If their senior pastor is a gifted teacher and administrator, then they receive the joy of having a pastor who

9. The most notable lists are found in 1 Cor 12 and Rom 12.

10. I say "gifts" plural on purpose. I am convinced that God gives most of us multiple spiritual gifts.

11. 1 Cor 12.

teaches well and offers great direction in administrative pursuits. Yet, they miss out on having pastoral leadership gifted in areas such as service, mercy, hospitality, leadership, and more.

However, in a plural elder polity, the church is led by multiple men—each with a unique set of gifts—and this means the church's pastoral leadership is literally more gifted. The church benefits not only from the gifts given to one man but from the gifts given to multiple men. The range and variety of spiritual gifts given to their pastoral leadership is not confined to the giftedness of one man. If their senior pastor is a gifted teacher, their associate pastor is a gifted administrator, one lay elder is gifted in hospitality, and another lay elder is gifted in leadership, then the church receives the blessing of being shepherded by all these gifts collectively. This is a gift to the body, as they get to experience the fullness of being led by men who are specifically gifted in so many various areas![12]

This benefit is right beside "more hands" as one of the most practical benefits. These two are probably the ones that are easiest to see and feel. So, take the time to help your fellow members understand spiritual gifts (if they don't already). Then, after they do, help them see this benefit and how it could be expanded by having more pastors.

PERSONAL EXPERIENCE

My giftedness and strengths lie mainly in teaching, administration, and complementary areas of leadership. The church has often shown appreciation for these things, and I find great joy when I can focus more fully on them. If I'm being honest, for years, the church didn't benefit as much from mercy, hospitality, or exhortation as it should have.

However, I am currently serving alongside two other pastors, Don and Adam. Don is very gifted at mercy, service, and hospitality. He spent the previous several decades

12. It is also a gift to you, as it allows you to focus more time and energy on your areas of greatest gifting, and serving where we are gifted is a truly joyful experience!

> serving the church as a deacon, and doing so well! He loves to sit on the front porch with a member to hear their stories and pray with them. He and his wife are retired and often go together to make such visits, and the body has begun to benefit significantly from these particular gifts.
>
> Adam is gifted in multiple areas that overlap with my giftings, but he is particularly more gifted than I am in exhortation. He feels very comfortable (and often compelled) to approach a member who is not living a life consistent with the word of God and point that out to them. He does not mind asking someone to come into the office and sit down with them to talk about a particular post on social media or a habit that has come to his attention. This is needed in every church, and I'm thankful God has given us a pastor who is exceptionally gifted in this area.
>
> MZBC is a healthier church that is more well cared for and more fully shepherded because I am not doing it alone. We have a more gifted leadership team than we did before, and I believe that honors God because—after all—the gifts came from him!

Though spiritual gifting is a more theological concept, its expression in the life of the church is practical in many ways. It allows the church to be more comprehensively built up and spiritually mature.[13] Spiritual maturity will lead to desires such as increased accountability and pastoring for every member, which are the next two benefits offered by a plural elder polity.

Benefit 4: Additional Accountability

Aim: The congregation will see that adding elders will offer greater accountability and protection to the elders and the body.

13. Eph 4.

There is another well-known adage that says, "Power tends to corrupt; absolute power corrupts absolutely."[14] This adage has proven true in the lives of many dictators, some CEOs, and, unfortunately, in the lives of several pastors as well.

Giving one man unmatched authority and unchecked power is a recipe for disaster, yet this is often found in many single pastor churches. The pastor is frequently viewed as "untouchable" as long as what he does is not illegal or grossly immoral. This is, in part, due to the fact that most members feel uncomfortable going to a pastor to discuss matters of sin, such as being short-tempered with his wife, being lazy in his scheduling, or being unprepared as a leader. Pastors are often perceived as unapproachable by many members, which means that many pastors lack a system of accountability within their local church. Help the congregation understand that this pattern is dangerous.

However, in a plural elder polity, biblical accountability for all members—including each pastor—is built into the fabric of the system. Acts 20:28 tells us that part of a pastor's job is to "pay careful attention to yourselves and to all the flock." Therefore, if there are multiple pastors, then part of their job is to offer accountability to one another. This means there is no individual in the church who is above all others. There is no man who does not have a local overseer. No one is exempt from being directly held accountable by other pastors.

This is a major benefit to the pastor, who now enjoys the good and godly gift of biblical accountability. He is safeguarded against sin and temptation, but more pertinent to most members, the church is safeguarded against the possibility of a domineering pastor.

Let me share a couple of hypothetical scenarios that help display this truth. Consider using these, or similar scenarios, when explaining this benefit to the church.

14. Encyclopædia Britannica, "John Emerich Edward Dalberg Acton."

Hypothetical Scenario 1

You begin exhibiting a pattern of sinful behavior. This isn't something grossly immoral like cheating on your wife, but something more acceptable like being lazy and not regularly going to the office to study and prepare, or being overly harsh with your kids at the ballfield.

Imagine this scenario as a single pastor. It is unlikely that there are members in your church who will feel comfortable coming to you to point out your sin and recommend a course correction. This lack of accountability could lead to a compounding of your laziness or continued trauma for your children.

Let's imagine the same scenario in a church where you are pastoring alongside other elders. In that scenario, these men, who are seen (by the body, themselves, and you) as being your equal, and who are specifically tasked with "paying careful attention to themselves and to all the flock"[15] are much more likely to feel comfortable asking about the pattern, recommending you correct the issue, and pointing out that it is sinful and unacceptable.

Hypothetical Scenario 2

You feel there is a major change needed; maybe the church needs a new building, needs to replace the chairman of a particular committee, or needs to change the music it sings. However, you are the only one who sees this need and find yourself becoming frustrated because the church doesn't see what you see.

In a single pastor setting, it is possible that you could begin to "throw your weight around" and use your influence to push for the thing you want unduly. You could bully someone out of a position or seek to control the situation unilaterally. After all, you are *the* pastor.

However, in a setting where you are one of the pastors, there are other men who have the same level of authority as you. Even if you, from a position of lead or senior pastor, seek to usurp them and gain unfair control of a situation, the body has a direct

15. Acts 20:28.

recourse for protection. They have multiple pastors, and those pastors have authority over you, which allows them to handle the situation much more quickly and adequately.

Recognize this, brothers. There are many in the church who have been deeply wounded by unfaithful shepherds. They have seen domineering men, lazy men, and sinful men serving as pastors and have been hurt by them in very sinful ways.

Highlighting how these problems are more probable in a single pastor polity and less likely in a plural elder polity can have a significant personal impact on these members. Take the time to help them see how having multiple pastors offers accountability to the pastor and protection to the body, and many will immediately desire this shift.

PERSONAL EXPERIENCE

While there have been no instances of pastoral accountability or correction during my time at MZBC, I can assure you that if Don and Adam were to come to me and share that they both felt I was being domineering, unfair, or living in a way that is out of step with Scripture's teachings, it would carry great weight. I know those brothers take the word and their calling seriously, and I am thankful for that.

I also know there was a time—years before I came—when a pastor was acting like a bully. He was eventually confronted (by deacon leaders) and stopped, but the process was much less smooth and took more time because there was no one in the church directly tasked with overseeing and bringing accountability to the pastor. If there had been multiple pastors, I believe the situation would have been rectified more smoothly and quickly, and the church would have been protected in a greater way.

Accountability and a clear path for course correction are both integral parts of a healthy church. Another integral part of a healthy church is healthy pastoral leadership, which is of great benefit to every single member of the church. Let's see how this can be more comprehensively offered by a plural elder polity.

Benefit 5: Panoramic Pastoring

Aim: The congregation will see that adding elders will ensure that every member—including the pastors—has a pastor to care for them.

I am convinced that—when striving to reach the full level of spiritual maturity God intends for us—church members greatly benefit from healthy pastoral leadership.[16] Put in another way, all church members—all Christians—need pastoral care and leadership.

One thing that can often be overlooked in such thinking is that pastors are themselves church members. Yes, they hold a particular office in the church, but at the end of the day, they are also members in need of guidance and care. In his book on elders, Jeremy Rinne says this to pastors, "But in the midst of all this shepherd-speak, remember a complementary truth: you are still sheep yourselves."[17] He goes on to describe this as a "great paradox" in which every pastor is both a "shepherd of sheep" and a "follower of Jesus."[18]

If you agree with the premises listed above—that all members need pastoral care, and that pastors are members—then we can also agree on this fact: *pastors need pastors*. Writing about this, Dave Harvey says, "Leaders need gifted people around them, a team that will demonstrate God's love through care, collaboration, and the scalpel of mutual accountability."[19] Every pastor needs

16. I would build this argument on passages like Jer 3:15, Eph 4:11–15, Col 1:28–29, Heb 13:17, and 1 Pet 5:1–5.

17. Rinne, *Church Elders*, 83.

18. Rinne, *Church Elders*, 83.

19. Harvey, *Plurality Principle*, 84.

men who will not only hold them accountable but will walk with them through difficult times, pray for them when they are sick, mentor them, give oversight to their lives, care for their families, and nurture them in the ways pastors do.[20]

Help the congregation see how this particular challenge is intensified in a single pastor polity and mollified in a plural elder polity.

In a single pastor church, there is no one to pastor the pastor. Sure, he can look to an AMS or another local pastor. This is certainly better than nothing, but having a pastor who isn't part of your local body is like having a shepherd living in another field. It simply doesn't work well. Listen to these two quotes from Dave Harvey about this truth: "Let's face it. If a pastor's accountability isn't from men in his local church, it's probably not real accountability."[21] "True care starts with those who know us best—those closest to us, those who know us well enough to track our joys and temptations."[22] In this polity, the pastor is left to care for himself. He misses out on many of the joys of pastoral leadership and care experienced by other members, and oftentimes, his family does, too.

However, in a church with multiple pastors, every pastor has other men who care for him in this way. He has men dedicated to his spiritual growth, the health of his family, the sharpening of his skills, and the care for his soul. He has men who hold him accountable and walk with him through difficult times. Each pastor gets to experience the richness of pastoral leadership and care experienced by all other members!

20. Newton says, "Pastors struggle with the same discipline, obedience, humility, and spiritual challenges facing members of their congregations." Newton, "How to Pastor One Another," para. 3.

21. Harvey, *Plurality Principle*, 88.

22. Harvey, *Plurality Principle*, 85.

PERSONAL EXPERIENCE

I have personally benefited from this very principle. I have had things I needed to seek counsel on that I was able to take to Don and Adam. I knew these brothers would pray with me, pray for me, and offer me fair feedback, and they did. Not only that, but they ensure I take adequate time off and care for my wife and kids, ensuring they are also being pastored by men other than their husband/father. They have been a great gift to me, and I'm thankful they are in my life.

This particular point was also an important one in our transition process. This is one of the principles that, once presented to the church, really seemed to resonate with them. They genuinely care for me, and when they realized I was missing out on all the benefits of pastoral ministry they were enjoying, they immediately felt moved to help alleviate what was lacking there.

The Bible is clear: for churches and church members to be all God intends for them to be, they need healthy pastoral leadership. This is more comprehensively offered by a plural elder polity. However, the office of pastor/elder is not the only important office in the church. Let's consider how a plural elder polity benefits the other office: the office of deacon.

Benefit 6: Distinct Deacons

Aim: The congregation will see that adding elders frees up deacons to focus on the diaconal ministry assigned to them in the New Testament.

There are two offices in the New Testament church: pastor/elder/overseer[23] and deacon. These two offices have distinct names,

23. These are not three separate offices, but three titles given to the one

qualifications, and functions, but their tasks are inseparable. Both offices are necessary for a church to reach its full potential. In order to operate properly and efficiently, pastors need deacons to serve, and deacons need pastors to lead.[24]

However, in many single pastor churches, there is a significant amount of overlap in the duties of these two offices. In such a polity, deacons often function as pseudo-elders, governing various areas of church life, teaching in multiple settings, and being called to shepherd a portion of the congregation. In these churches, it is very common to see the deacons acting as a second ruling arm that affords a "check and balance" system to the pastor.

To be fair, I believe that many churches with this model just barely missed the mark. They were "so close, yet so far." Oftentimes, this polity is employed to meet the need for plural leadership. I believe many such churches recognize the need for accountability and care, can see that there is too much work for one man to do alone, and know that no individual is adequately gifted to fulfill all the tasks given to church leaders. They see this need and come oh-so-close to the prevalent New Testament model of plural eldership. They recognize the need for plurality, but instead of seeing this need and saying, "We need more pastors," they look at it and decide, "We should have the deacons fill some of these pastoral duties."

There are two reasons why this model is gravely concerning. Neither of these is likely to be obvious to most people, so you will once again need to take time to educate the body on these truths. However, I believe when they understand them, they will more deeply desire a plural elder polity.

---

office. We often use the term "pastor," but the Bible uses these three terms synonymously. For more, see Merkle, *40 Questions*.

24. In Acts 6, we see the relationship between the apostles and the seven chosen men. However, this is widely accepted as a prototype structure depicting the future relationship between pastors and deacons. For more, see Smethurst, *Deacons*, or Anyabwile, *Finding Faithful Elders and Deacons*.

1. When deacons serve as pastors, they are fulfilling tasks and duties for which they are neither called nor qualified.

The truth is that the two offices are separate for a reason. Deacons are never tasked with oversight,[25] teaching,[26] or shepherding.[27] Therefore, when you take a deacon who is not set apart for such tasks and ask him to do them, you have set him up to fail. You are asking them to fulfill tasks and duties the Lord has not prepared or called them to fill. To task deacons with doing pastoral ministry is to stray from the design of the New Testament church.

2. When deacons serve as pastors, no one serves as a deacon.

Have you ever seen a church where there simply didn't seem to be anyone focused on service? There were numerous administrators and "chefs in the kitchen," but no one was responsible for caring for widows and orphans, overseeing property care, or addressing practical needs. I would venture a guess that this was likely a church with a single pastor. This is not always the case. There are churches with plural elder leadership that are weak in service ministry, and there are single pastor churches that excel in it. However, the pattern I have seen most often is one where deacons are asked to fill the role of pastor, and therefore, no one ends up filling the office of deacon.

Help the congregation to understand that in a single elder model, the deacons (or some other non-pastor) will almost always be tasked with fulfilling pastoral duties. The only true options are for non-pastors to come alongside the pastor in fulfilling these duties, or for many of them to remain undone. Most often, the non-pastors who receive these assignments are deacons. When that happens, deacons serve as pastors, and diaconal ministry falls to the wayside.

25. The office of pastor is called "overseer" multiple times in the New Testament; the office of deacon never is.

26. This is the most obvious omission between the qualifications of pastors and deacons.

27. The word "pastor" literally means to shepherd. For more, see Bingham and Parsons, "What Is the Difference."

However, in a plural elder polity, there are multiple pastors who can work together to fulfill the pastoral tasks and duties. This allows the deacons to be relieved of such duties, allowing them to focus on the diaconal ministry assigned to them. In this model, the pastoral duties are fulfilled by pastors, and the diaconal ministry is fulfilled by deacons, and both of these patterns are biblical and desirable.

PERSONAL EXPERIENCE

At MZBC, the first lay pastor we recognized was Don Hollis, a man who had faithfully served as a deacon for decades. The truth is, Don had done much more than serve as a deacon. He had been standing with one foot in each office for years and years. Don had served as chairman of almost every vital committee we had, held many things together in between pastors, taught in almost every possible setting, and shepherded members both individually and corporately.

Given MZBC's limited number of active deacons, it was a significant burden on the deacon ministry to ask Don to handle all these tasks. The deacon ministry suffered because Don was asked to fill an office he wasn't in. If it were only one man, then this might not have seemed too big a deal, but Don isn't the only deacon who was asked to serve in pastoral capacities.

Since shifting to a plural elder polity and bringing Don on as a pastor, the church has been able to delineate between the two offices more clearly. With multiple men serving as pastors, we no longer need to ask deacons to fill these capacities. This affords a full complement of deacons to attend to the practical, service, and mercy ministries of the church, allowing them to focus their attention fully on these duties. This has been good for the church in almost every way!

Clearly, a plural elder polity is a benefit to the body by benefitting both the office of pastor and the office of deacon. One final benefit I believe is important to mention is that having a plural elder polity ensures greater health and ministry during times of pastoral transition. Let's consider how this polity will practically benefit the body during such times.

Benefit 7: Stronger Succession

Aim: The congregation will see that adding elders allows the church to have a stronger leadership team during times of pastoral transition.

One of the great things about being a pastor is that your overarching job description does not change. Whether you are a staff elder or lay elder, whether you have a more specific designation (associate pastor, youth pastor, etc.) or not, the Bible still tasks you with the same role of shepherding the church.

There are particular giftings and unique areas of focus, but the work of providing oversight, vision, congregational care, equipping the saints, teaching, etc., does not change. This is particularly beneficial during one of the most tumultuous times in the life of a church: seasons of pastoral transition.

Every church hates to hear the news that its senior pastor is leaving. During these interim times, churches usually see a significant drop in attendance and often choose to set aside many ministry or mission efforts. That is because such things are often led and directed by pastors.

In a single pastor model, the absence of a senior pastor means there is no pastoral leadership. Sure, the church will seek an interim, but he will typically only cover the task of teaching/preaching. Therefore, directions for missions and ministry, as well as the pursuit of hiring new staff and long-range planning, are put on hold. This can be crippling for a church.

However, in a church with multiple elders, particularly when some of them are lay elders, the church is ensured to have pastoral guidance and care even in the absence of a senior pastor. This polity allows the church to have dedicated, recognized, and trained men at the helm still steering the ship, and ensuring that vision is still cast, members are still shepherded, equipped, and cared for, and ministry continues without interruption.

PERSONAL EXPERIENCE

At this point, MZBC has yet to deal with a pastoral succession while having a plural elder polity. I have been able to continue serving as the senior pastor, and our only other staff pastor has remained in place as well. Therefore, we have not been able to experience this benefit personally.

However, I have made it a point to train the other elders—both staff and lay—on all aspects of pastoral ministry to prepare them for that day when it comes. It is my desire that they understand our philosophy of missions, oversight, leadership, how to guide committees and teams, how to care for our staff and members, and how to preach and teach.

Having trained, equipped, and recognized elders will ensure that during a time of pastoral transition, much more than preaching takes place. The elders will be able to meet with committees and teams, offering guidance and direction that will allow the ministry to persist unhindered. Missional engagement will remain cohesive, as the church will have elders in place who have personal relationships with our long-term mission partners and church plants around the world.

Alongside these missional and leadership roles, the elders will also be able to ensure that members are still shepherded. The members will still have pastors who know them personally to walk with them through difficulties and to celebrate with them in times of joy. None

> of the things assigned to pastoral leadership will be neglected, even during a time of pastoral transition.[28]

These seven benefits offered by a plural elder polity show the significant advantage this model has over a single elder polity. Some of the advantages are more theological in nature and some are more practical, but they are all beneficial to the local church and worthy of consideration!

CONCLUSION

Sick people go to the doctor. Hungry people look for something to eat. Why? Because people respond to felt needs.

At this point, you have helped the church understand its need; there is a deficiency in pastoral leadership. They see that no man can carry the weight of pastoral ministry alone and comprehensively complete the task.

However, helping them see their need is not enough; you also need to help them see the solution! A plurality of elders is not just a theoretical or theological idea but a proven model with practical benefits. This biblical model exalts Christ, spreads the workload, and brings greater accountability, care, and diversity of gifts to the pastoral ministry of the church.

So don't neglect this opportunity. Present this to them with excitement and clarity. Teach them with patience and help them see not only what they are missing but what they could be gaining!

Help them picture older members being visited and cared for, youth being shepherded, and every member being mentored more fully. Use concrete scenarios and hypothetical examples to help them envision this as the future of the church.

28. We took this benefit into account when rewriting our guiding documents. Though our lay elders have a rotation and sabbatical plan, there is a clause that states that all lay elders will remain active during times of pastoral transition.

I believe every church deserves the comprehensive pastoral care afforded by a plural eldership. The question is not whether this model will benefit the church, but whether you will lead them to see and embrace that vision.

Once you have completed this step, the next one will be to help the church envision how a plurality of elders will look in their own context. That is where we turn our attention in the next chapter, but for now, take courage and begin the work of leading toward this vision.

4

Casting Vision

Helping the Congregation Envision the Change

There it was, bare, simple, and plain. Needing something, but I had no idea what. The room where our youth met was a large, plain, and neutral-colored space. It was clear that the space needed something to make it feel warmer and more inviting; something to enhance its functionality, but I had no idea what it needed.

This is not an isolated event for me; I am terrible at trying to decorate or promote function through form. I look at a room, and I see a room. However, our youth pastor's wife came in and immediately saw a reclaimed wood wall, some rustic arrows, and other decorations that would warm the space beautifully.

Later, we hired an associate pastor who took it a step further by adding a small stage and lighting to enhance the space's functionality. Now, it is a warm, inviting, and fully functioning space where the youth regularly gather for Bible study and worship. Now, I can finally see what it needed all along!

But not at the beginning. I didn't have the vision; I couldn't picture what they pictured. This experience provided me with a profound understanding of one of the challenges leaders often face. They can easily see the finished product. The change, the transition, the restructuring is so clear that they can't miss it. However, the people they are leading can't, and that's where vision casting—helping others see what only you can see—comes in.

CASTING VISION

If you are going to lead a church in adopting a new polity, you will be required to cast a vision. That's because at this point, many of your fellow members are like me when I initially walked into that room. They have heard your teaching about a plural elder polity. They recognize that the current system isn't fulfilling its intended purpose and, therefore, needs to be changed. However, they have no idea what that change could look like.

Full disclosure: I used to hate the term "vision casting." It seemed so dramatic and overused. Leaders or pastors would often discuss the need for vision casting or their extraordinary ability to cast vision, and I wondered if they were simply trying to make themselves seem more important than they were. Then, I came to lead this transition and finally understood what this idea meant.

Leader, your fellow members are familiar with the idea of having one pastor, but the concept of having three, five, or nine seems utterly foreign to them. You see it; you know the form, the function, the beautiful gift it would be. You can picture all the rich blessings it would afford the church, but you may be the only one.

Your fellow members have never seen a church with this polity, and they can't picture it in this one either. This work can't be displayed on a canvas with brushes, so how do we begin sharing the beautiful picture in our head? For me, the first step is always the same—look to Scripture.

BEGIN WITH SCRIPTURE

This is always my default. God's word is the only infallible resource we have, and it happens to contain some great examples of multiple men serving alongside one another. You have already shown them that this idea is biblical, but now use examples from Scripture to help illustrate this practical idea for them.

You can point to the Jerusalem Council in Acts 15, where an important topic was considered. In that chapter, we see a gathering of apostles and elders, as well as various men with diverse gifts. We see Peter teaching, Barnabas and Paul testifying what they had seen and experienced, and James exhorting the others to agree with him.

There are other examples of divisions of labor throughout the New Testament as well, but by far, my favorite text to use when illustrating this point is Exod 18.

In Exod 18, the Israelites have been set free from Egyptian bondage, preserved through the Red Sea, provided for in the wilderness, and protected against enemies. They are establishing themselves as an organized people, and Moses is the judge of the nation. At this point, Moses was not only the senior leader of God's people but he was really serving as the only leader, and this was wearing him and everyone else out! We are told he sat in judgment with people around him "from morning till evening."[1] This appears to have been their typical pattern. People would stand in line for long periods, waiting to receive judgments from Moses and have their disputes settled by him alone. You can imagine how difficult this was for Moses and how frustrating for the people.[2]

One day, Jethro, Moses' father-in-law, came to town and observed this pattern. Immediately, he made this statement to Moses: "What you are doing is not good."[3] Jethro recommended that Moses appoint other men to help him in this task. Some would oversee large groups, and some would oversee small groups, but there would be a clear division of labor. Moses followed this advice, and the new plan was better for him and all the people of Israel.

1. Exod 18:13.

2. If you are a solo pastor, then you likely have a very personal understanding of the difficulty of Moses' task.

3. Exod 18:17.

PERSONAL EXPERIENCE

Clearly, this text was not meant to be a one-to-one correlation with a church shifting from a single elder polity to a plural elder polity. Nevertheless, it provides a clear picture of what this type of division can look like and lead to.

This text was instrumental in casting this vision at Mt. Zion. It paints a clear picture of one man doing all the work on his own, illustrating how this pattern both wears him out and frustrates the rest of the members. Then, it offers the biblical wisdom of dividing the labor between that one man and other qualified men, and the result is something beautiful and desirable. This text is one of the clearest pictures of what a shift to a plural elder polity can look like in a church.

After you have taught this, more members will understand it. However, not everyone is an auditory learner, and some who understand the scriptural basis will still need the concept fleshed out. That is where visual aids—such as charts, handouts, and diagrams—can really help them see the big picture.

VISUAL AIDS AND HANDOUTS

Some people are visual learners. They don't learn as well from lectures, but if you can offer them an illustration, an example, they've got it! You've probably encountered such people when playing card or board games before. You know the type, you read the instructions, and they look more confused than before. Then, you play one round while they watch, and they've got it!

There are almost certainly some of these people in the church where you are serving. They don't just need to hear about Moses and Jethro; they need to see a visualization of some sort. While it might be more difficult to find visual aids to go with a shift in polity, there are at least a few you can use (and many of you are more creative than me and likely have even more ideas).

Organizational Flow Chart

You can use an organizational chart (flow chart). If the shift you are proposing includes a restructuring of committees or staff tasks, you could prepare a handout that lists these changes in bullet or chart form, like the one seen here:

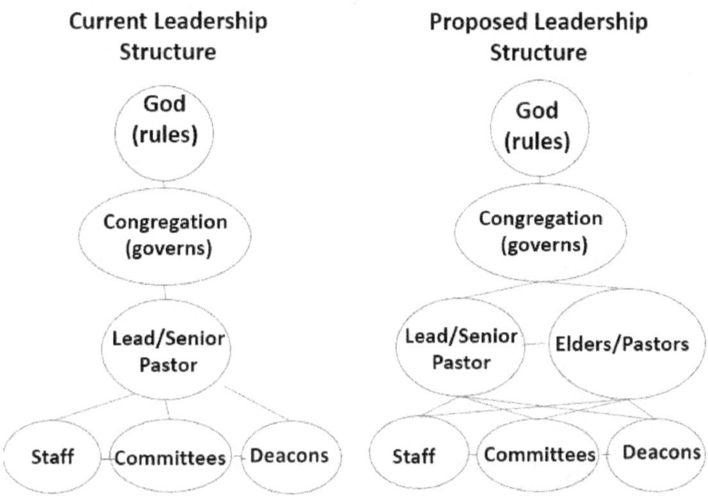

As you can see, this chart helps the congregation understand that the proposed addition of more elders will not diminish the role of the current senior pastor, nor will it abolish or discredit in any way congregational authority or the role of the staff, deacons, or committees.

This might be different in your local context. Perhaps the proposal you are recommending involves a significant reorganization of current leadership groups. Either way, a chart similar to this one can help the congregation understand where they are now and where you are proposing they go in the future.

Frequently Asked Questions Document

Another helpful tool you could create is a frequently asked questions (FAQ) handout that answers questions like "What is Polity? What is an Elder Polity? Do other churches in our denomination utilize this polity? If we choose to swap to this polity, will the authority of church members diminish?" I know you will likely answer all of these questions during your teaching sessions, but for some, a handout, list, or written description helps them process the information more fully.

You will want to ensure that this document covers the questions you are hearing, but it can also include ones you anticipate. If you would like to see an example, there is a sample page of what an FAQ document could look like in appendix A.

It can seem tedious to answer these questions multiple times in multiple settings, and creating a document like this one can reduce the number of times you have to do that. This also gives members a clear reference they can refer to repeatedly. One of the other great things about an FAQ document is that it allows you to answer the questions in your own words. This ensures the members hear your thoughts, rather than those of someone who might not have the correct answer.

PERSONAL EXPERIENCE

At Mt. Zion, the body had begun to grasp the theological idea of multiple men sharing authority. Still, they were struggling with questions like, "Who will the staff answer to? What changes will occur in the deacon ministry? Who will oversee the _________ ministry? How will the lay elders function on a day-in-day-out basis?" Therefore, we created a flowchart similar to the one found in this chapter.

We also created an FAQ document similar to the one found above to answer fifteen of the most frequently asked questions that arose during the early stages of this process. Both of these proved instrumental in helping the body become more fully comfortable with this shift in polity. Though it was a tedious process, it was praised by many members.

Both the flow chart and the FAQ document were helpful, but some people still wanted a fuller understanding of the practical role of lay pastors. Therefore, we turned our attention to another visual aid that the church was already familiar with: job descriptions.

LAY PASTOR JOB DESCRIPTIONS

Anyone who has ever started a new job knows the importance of a job description. These valuable tools help us understand what is expected of us, where to focus our time and attention, and what our assigned tasks and duties are.

When trying to help a congregation grasp the concept of having multiple pastors, you can use mock job descriptions for the same purpose. The members want to know what these men's duties will be, where they will focus their time and attention, and what will be expected of them, so write some job descriptions and offer them to the body to help illustrate this new role.

I recommend maintaining the same format used for your staff job descriptions—particularly if the congregation is already familiar with it. I also think it is helpful to go beyond simply listing duties. I recommend getting more granular and creating some hypothetical examples. Choose some names of men not found in your congregation, give each of them different strengths and giftings, and explain how each would function as part of the elder team. As an aid in the process, I have provided an example of what these mock job descriptions could look like in appendix B.

If you have members who have worked in HR, who are evaluated annually based on performance, or have served on your personnel committee, they are likely familiar with job descriptions.

This is just one more tool that can help assist the congregation to see what you see.

PERSONAL EXPERIENCE

I know I have mentioned this about other parts of the process, but I genuinely believe the mock job descriptions were one of the most valuable tools for us during this process. As the body struggled to envision having more than one pastor, we continually received this question: What would these men do?

To help answer that question, we created the mock job descriptions found in appendix B. These were hypothetical descriptions that utilized the same format as our staff job descriptions. The names and giftings were made up, but the descriptions allowed the congregation to see the role these men would fill in a practical and digestible format.

These handouts and visual aids were extremely helpful. The people were beginning to see how the lay pastors would interact with staff and what their practical ministry roles would be. However, they still had nagging questions that remained unanswered. To ensure everyone had an opportunity to ask these questions, we set aside time for open Q&A sessions.

QUESTION AND ANSWER SESSIONS

I am part of the planning team for the "Equip to Exposit" conference, an annual pastors' conference. Every year, we bring in a scholar who has published a commentary and have him walk us through the book of the Bible he wrote about.

One of the most exciting aspects of this conference is that we bring in scholars who are gifted lecturers, but we also ensure they are willing to take questions from the floor throughout their teaching!

If I'm sitting in my office reading a commentary, and I want to know more about how the author came to a certain conclusion, I'm out of luck. However, during the conference, I am able to simply ask the brother, "What made you draw that conclusion?"

The same thing can be true of church members. They can hear us teach about a plural elder polity and still have questions about how we came to a certain point or thought. They can read every handout and memorize every visual aid but still have gaps in their understanding.

That's why I recommend you consider holding open Q&A sessions. These sessions provide members with the opportunity to sit down with you, pick your brain, ask questions they've been wanting to ask, and hear others' questions as well. One of the great things about this tool is that it allows you to address the questions and concerns the body has, not just the ones you think they might have.[4]

During these sessions, I was able to directly address concerns like, "Do we have any men in our church who meet the qualifications to pastor, or is this just theoretical?" I was also asked, "Are you doing this in order to get a certain man elected as a pastor? Do you have a particular individual or individuals in mind for this role?" There were also some concerns over the perceived ties between reformed/Calvinistic theology and this change that I was able to address.

Each time I answered one of these questions openly and honestly, it helped members formulate a more comprehensive and honest view of a plural elder polity. This is the goal; helping them see what they can't see, and this was one more tool to help me do that.

4. A word of caution here. These meetings can get contentious at times. If you know there are very vocal members who strongly oppose this change, you might be better off offering extended "office hours" for members to come by and ask questions. Alternatively, you can ask that questions be submitted beforehand, and you can then answer them live at a town hall–style setting.

PERSONAL EXPERIENCE

At MZBC, we offered multiple Q&A sessions, typically on Wednesday nights before services or on Sunday afternoons. The crowd was usually small—only those who had questions came—but that was fitting. They wouldn't last more than thirty minutes or so, and I was able to offer a lot of really needed direction. In fact, these sessions brought out several concerns that I had not perceived or anticipated.

Alongside these church-wide meetings, I also held individual Q&A sessions with groups like our deacons. I found that some people are more likely to ask a question in a more intimate setting.

However you decide to go about hosting these town hall meetings or Q&A sessions, I recommend you do so. The members of MZBC seemed particularly thankful for the opportunity to be heard and addressed, and I believe your fellow members will as well.

You might ask which of these tools—the flow chart, FAQ document, job descriptions, or Q&A sessions—was most useful. I can't answer that question because each one helped bring clarity to a different group of people. Honestly, it was the sum total of all of them that helped produce a clear vision for the congregation.

Let's end by looking at this process from a ten-thousand-foot view.

CONCLUSION

As a leader, we should not see others' lack of vision as a frustration but as an opportunity. When they see nothing, you have the opportunity to paint the picture you want them to see. It's like me and that youth room. When I saw it, I saw nothing. No plans, no ideas. I had no expectation of what the improvements would be. This meant that those around me had the opportunity to start from scratch and help me see what they wanted me to see—what they wanted the room to become. This principle also applies to leading a congregation to consider a new polity.

This is where you are now. You have the vision of what this polity will look like, and the church does not. You have a blank canvas before you, and you can begin painting the picture you desire them to see! This process is what we call "casting vision."

When it comes to casting vision, the well-known Christian leadership expert John Maxwell says this: "The response will be determined by two things. By the message, in other words, what's being said. And the messenger, who is saying it."[5] As we conclude this chapter, I would like to use these two categories to help us remember what we are doing and why.

The first thing he addresses is the message. You know the message; you are articulating the biblical pattern of multiple men pastoring a single church. This message is sound, but just because it is sound does not mean that it is automatically understood. Remember, just because something is clear to you doesn't mean it is clear to the others around you.

It is your job to take this vision and to cast—or explain—it in a way that allows the congregation to see this biblical pattern in contemporary practice. You want them to have a clear understanding of what this polity would look like in the day-to-day world of their local church. You will know you have done this when people begin to ask questions like, "When do we get started?" or "What is the next step?" rather than, "What will these men do?" or "Why do we need this?"

As you go through this process, look for such indicators. Pay attention to the questions people are asking and look for a shift that indicates they finally see it and are ready to move forward. From time to time, stop and ask yourself, "Can the body clearly articulate what a plural elder polity is, how it would benefit us, and what these men would do?" If the answer is no, then you aren't ready to move forward.

5. Maxwell, "Leader-Vision," para. 11.

The second thing Maxwell mentioned was the messenger. Let this be a reminder that while *what* is being said is important, so is *who* is saying it and *how* they are saying it. You are not a salesman trying to sell people on a product or a CEO attempting to pressure a board into agreement. You are a pastor who is faithfully shepherding God's flock by patiently offering clarity to people you love! Vision casting is not the same thing for you as it is for an executive.

This process will likely be more tedious and lengthier than you expect. Helping people visualize something they have never seen before is challenging, but it is valuable. This is an opportunity for you to present the church with a vision of the future, and to do so in a way that demonstrates that you love them more than you love your vision. During this transition, I regularly said, "If we never get there. If Mt. Zion never decides to transition to this polity, then I will gladly continue to pastor here as long as the Lord will allow."

Vision casting can be challenging, especially if you're new to the process. If this is you, then don't feel like you have no hope. There is a specific tool that will help you in the process, and it is what we will discuss in the next chapter: a lead team.

5

Mobilizing Others

Working with Lead Teams and Trusted Voices

When it comes to leading change, one instrument every leader should seek to use is the power of influence. Let me offer a personal example of how powerful this tool can be.

I can still remember seeing it for the first time. I was eleven years old, and I saw one of the most iconic commercials I have ever seen. It was a Gatorade commercial featuring Michael Jordan and Mia Hamm. Now, I am old enough to be in the "Michael Jordan is the greatest basketball player of all time" camp, and at the time, Mia Hamm was a household name.

Needless to say, when a commercial featuring these two iconic figures came on, I paid attention![1] It featured the two athletes competing in various sports and activities, and of course, they were drinking Gatorade the whole time. As an eleven-year-old kid, you can bet your bottom dollar this sold me on drinking Gatorade!

1. This was the iconic "Anything you can do, I can do better" commercial. Weisholz, "Michael Jordan, Mia Hamm."

THE POWER OF INFLUENCE

Why do I tell you all of that? To highlight the power of influence. Sure, Gatorade could have had a nutritionist in their commercial explaining electrolytes and how they help replenish what is lost in sweat. Or they could have had their CEO say he recommended I start drinking Gatorade to improve my athletic performance. But neither would have had the same effect. For me, the decision to begin drinking Gatorade had nothing to do with science or nutrition and everything to do with these two influential athletes!

Companies and corporations spend billions of dollars every year on advertising and spokespersons. They have entire departments dedicated to identifying the right people and conveying the right message. You know why? Because influence is a powerful tool that works. It's crucial to recognize this when seeking to convince people to make a change in their lives!

Just as Gatorade chose two iconic athletes to represent their brand and product, you should consider utilizing the influential voices of others to help shape the congregation's view of a plural elder polity.

This might sound a bit icky and inappropriate when discussing leading God's people toward biblical change. Believe me, there are some inappropriate ways to go about it. However, influence is not inherently bad; it can be used appropriately, and when applied correctly, influence can be a powerful and effective tool to help lead significant change in a church.

So, if influence is such a powerful tool in both marketing and ministry, how can you utilize it to help lead a change in polity? This chapter will introduce two distinct avenues that enable you to effectively and appropriately use the influence of others in leading this change.

The first is a lead team, which is a strong tool that will influence multiple levels of this process. For that reason, we will spend most of our time thinking about it. I will define and describe it and also help you think through the process of selecting, training, and utilizing one.

The second tool I will recommend is trusted testimonies. This avenue is less complex but can be equally powerful. I will help you see the effectiveness of these trusted testimonies, offer diagnostic questions to help identify the right individuals to give them, and share how we did this at MZBC.

Let's begin by examining the concept of a lead team.

THE INFLUENCE OF OTHERS—UTILIZING A LEAD TEAM

Let's begin by defining what a lead team is. A lead team is simply what it sounds like: a group of knowledgeable and trusted advisors who serve alongside the pastor in leading a change. The president of the United States has a cabinet of trusted advisors. Fortune 500 companies have diverse boards of directors, football teams have coordinators and advisors galore, and I believe a pastor seeking to lead a change in polity should have a trusted team of advisors as well. I refer to this group as the lead team.

A lead team fills multiple roles. *They influence the pastor* by offering differing perspectives. They also shore up his weaknesses. They help him identify potential points of resistance and evaluate timing. They also offer honest counsel and consider perspectives he may not be cognizant of. *They also influence the congregation*, using the years of trust they have built to help convince their fellow members that this change is worthwhile. When utilized properly, a lead team will be a valuable resource. It will significantly increase your chances of successfully leading a change. Now that we understand what a lead team is and its value to this process, we must consider one of the most pivotal aspects of any lead team: its members.

Having the wrong team members can severely hinder your ability to evaluate the process properly and can actually undermine the congregation's trust in this change. However, having the right ones will offer strategic planning, build momentum, and buy immediate trust from the congregation. Let's consider several aspects to help identify the right team.

Selecting the Right Team

The Right Team to Influence You

Any of you who have taken an Anatomy and Physiology course from a good teacher have probably had the experience of learning about your blind spot. Whether you know it or not, the spot where your optic nerve connects to your retina causes you to have a blind spot—a literal place where you cannot see.[2] When an object is located in your blind spot, it is still there, but you can't detect it.

When it comes to leading, we all have blind spots as well. Leadership blind spots don't come from an anatomical feature but from a lack of perspective. For example, I am a thirty-nine-year-old white male. Therefore, I don't have the same perspective as a woman, a senior adult, or any other minority group. I have only been a member of my church for seven years and therefore don't have the same perspective as a long-time member.

The fact that my experience and perspective are limited reveals the reality that I have blind spots. Other members likely have different questions and concerns that I do not share and might not have ever even considered. These things are real and present, but simply out of my field of view. Therefore, these are blind spots for me.

It is imperative that you address these gaps in perspective, but that's pretty difficult to do on your own (hence the term "blind spots"). One major advantage of having the right lead team is that they will help fill these gaps for you. If you choose team members who possess a different perspective from yours, they can help fill in your blind spots by offering insight and understanding you lack.

Therefore, it is imperative that you don't simply choose a bunch of your friends who look, think, and talk like you. That type of lead team might be affirming, but they will not be advantageous.

Below, I have compiled a list of potential demographics that are likely present in your church, each offering a potentially different perspective on a change in polity. Read through the list to

2. If you've never tested this, you should give it a try. Google "test to find your blind spot," and you can easily find instructions.

help identify your blind spots. After recognizing your blind spots, begin compiling a list of faithful and trustworthy church members. Focus on members who can provide the perspectives you lack. We will narrow this list further as we go, so feel free to begin with all the potential candidates who meet these criteria.

Perspectives to Consider

- Gender
- Age
- Socioeconomic status
- Ethnicity
- Years of membership
- Family status (kids, no kids; married, single)
- Educational background

You don't have to select individuals from every one of these subpopulations, and you may consider some not listed here; however, the more perspectives that can be represented, the better. Let's take just a moment to consider why it is important to consider different demographic perspectives when leading a major change.

In my case, as a thirty-nine-year-old white male who is married with five kids, there are a lot of questions I am likely to overlook. Senior adults in the congregation are more likely to be interested in learning about the role of a lay elder in congregational care or visitation ministry. Long-term members are likely more interested in understanding how lay elders will contribute to maintaining continuity between senior pastors, and mothers are more likely to have questions about the role of lay elders in children's ministry. So, identify the perspectives represented in the church that you currently lack, and try to add members who hold those views.

Another important aspect of a lead team is the team's size. How many members should your team have?

I believe the ideal team size is small enough to meet regularly, but large enough to fill in the necessary gaps, likely between three and seven members. Looking at the list above, you might think every team will need at least seven members, but that isn't necessarily true. If you are a young male, you can choose a seventy-five-year-old female and hit two birds with one stone.

No matter what size team you land on, I pray you recognize the importance of having a diverse lead team that can influence you during this process. They will help you see things you currently do not see. They'll address concerns you have never had before and add sensitivity to perspectives you lack. They will reveal hidden mines to you, invaluably strengthening your thought process. Do not neglect the task of selecting the right team to guide you.

PERSONAL EXPERIENCE

At Mt. Zion, I selected a lead team consisting of five individuals. The team was comprised of three males and two females. Two of the members had reached retirement age (I'm not guessing ages), and the other three ranged in age from forty-something to sixty-something. Two had been coaches, one worked in a hospital, one taught at a local community college, and one was a farmer. All of them had been members for over twenty years, and I will explain why in the following section. One had children still in the home, others had grown children and grandchildren in the church, and some had grown children who had moved away.

Having such a vast array of perspectives gave me confidence that no specific demographic within our congregation would feel unseen or unheard during this process. They offered me feedback and posed questions that proved to be invaluable during the transition. I trust that much of the success of the transition was due to their influence on me.

Selecting a team that could comprehensively cover my blind spots was an important aspect of choosing a lead team; however, it wasn't the only aspect to be considered. Let's consider how to select a lead team that can also influence the congregation during this process.

The Right Team to Influence the Congregation

The first vital role of the lead team is to influence you by offering advice, direction, and guidance. Their second significant role is to offer influence to the congregation.

Identifying Recognizable Members

As we consider individuals who fit this category, we recognize the importance of selecting team members who are well-known to the congregation. If you only choose team members who serve in the background, or if you choose new members whom most of the church doesn't know, the team's influence will be greatly diminished.

Think back on Gatorade's decision to pay Michael Jordan and Mia Hamm to be in their commercial. Why would they choose these two athletes? Why don't companies choose the third-string quarterback to be in their sports drink commercial? Why wouldn't a potato chip company choose Zach Kilpatrick to star in their Super Bowl commercial? Because star athletes and recognizable actors are well-known. Companies choose faces and names that people will recognize, as their popularity enhances their influence.

Again, we aren't trying to sell a product to anyone, but we do want to consider the significant impact the right lead team can have on the congregation. If you choose individuals who are well-known, then they will have an influence over a larger portion of the congregation. However, choosing individuals who are less recognizable will diminish the team's influence.

Consider finding individuals who fit the following criteria:

- Have served as head of a committee or team
- Are regularly before the body on Sundays
- Have taught classes of adults
- Lead certain ministries in the church
- Long-time members

Choosing individuals who fit these criteria will ensure you are picking members who will be recognizable to the congregation. Take the list you began earlier, the one with individuals from differing subpopulations, and narrow it based on these criteria. Then, let's narrow that list even further by considering members who aren't only recognizable but are also trustworthy.

Identifying Trustworthy Members

Many people take medications for high blood pressure while knowing absolutely nothing about the companies that develop and sell these products. They have no idea who the CEO is or what scientists produced the medicines. They don't know how the medicines are tested. For all intents and purposes, they are completely ignorant of the companies that produce the medicine. However, these individuals pay thousands of dollars for the medications and take them daily.

Why would millions of people put so much trust in a product they know little about from a company they know nothing about?

Judging from our previous section, you might think it is because these companies use recognizable celebrities in their commercials, but that isn't it. No, the key to their influence isn't someone who is well-known but someone trusted inherently.

The people taking these medications have great trust in their cardiologist. They don't often know the cardiologist well; they only see them during appointments. They don't have deep personal relationships with these physicians, but they trust them inherently because of the expertise and ability these individuals have displayed.

This illustration represents another key characteristic of a good lead team member: trustworthiness. They aren't required to hold a seminary degree that would establish them as a subject-area expert, but they do need to demonstrate a level of spiritual maturity, credibility, and character that would lead the congregation to trust them.

Even if church members aren't familiar with you or the elder polity you recommend, a lead team of trusted and respected individuals can help build their confidence in this change. Choosing members whom they have known for decades, who have sat in Sunday school rooms and hospital waiting rooms with them, and who have offered them sound advice about difficult situations will produce inherent trust in this process.

Consider the following criteria to help you find members that will likely be trustworthy and respected by the congregation:

- Strong Christian character
- Lead their family well
- Highly respected
- Good Bible teachers
- Proven servants or leaders
- Beloved members

Once again, revisit that list of potential lead team members and narrow it by these criteria. At this point, you should have a list of individuals who can help eliminate blind spots by considering questions and concerns the body will have, as well as the information you need to share during the education process. These individuals are also well-known to the congregation, trusted, and respected.

If you identify a handful of individuals who meet all these criteria and assemble them as a lead team, then you will gain great confidence from the church. Having a team like this allows you to gain influence you wouldn't have on your own—the influence of a lead team!

PERSONAL EXPERIENCE

At MZBC, all five lead team members had a reputation as individuals who possessed high Christian character. They were respected in the church and community, having proven their commitment and character over many years. Additionally, all five of them were well-known leaders within the body. The group consisted of our financial bookkeeper, three small group leaders/Sunday school teachers, three deacons, one deacon officer, our church treasurer, a greeter, and a minister's wife.[3]

There is no doubt in my mind that their influence is one reason Mt. Zion was able to make the change smoothly and successfully.

A Word of Warning About Selecting Lead Team Members

One thing I cannot stress strongly enough is the necessity of choosing men and women who have a high Christian character. There will likely be a temptation to choose at least one individual who is so-so on this scale, but please don't.

I know there is probably a well-known, charismatic man whose smile and charm would be a huge asset to such a team. However, if you know he isn't trustworthy, don't include him on the lead team.

There may also be a temptation to add someone whose character you don't know well to ensure you check all the subpopulation boxes. Maybe you can't think of a young mother or an older man of strong character. Instead of leaving out this demographic

3. I recognize these numerous roles seem to reflect more than five members. However, some of the lead team members filled multiple roles (such as Gwyn, who overlapped as our church treasurer, a deacon, and a Sunday school teacher).

perspective, you will be tempted to add a member whose Christian character is uncertain, but please don't.

It is better to lack perspective on your lead team than to lack spiritual maturity in it.

Remember, these individuals will have an influence on you. They will offer perspectives and thoughts that will change the way you lead this transition. More than that, they will influence the congregation! You are placing this person in a place of influence and leadership. When recommending what we look for in Christian leaders, the apostle Paul (under the inspiration of the Holy Spirit) did not mention charisma, charm, smile, speaking ability, or any other worldly thing. No, he talked about character, reputation, and trustworthiness.[4] I believe we should follow this pattern when selecting a lead team.[5]

Selecting the proper lead team is one of the most crucial aspects of this process, and one that should be approached with prayer and wisdom. After the proper team is in place, it is time to begin training them and employing them in this process.

Training and Utilizing a Lead Team

Before putting the newly selected team "in the field" to begin working, ensure you are all on the same page. It is your responsibility to ensure they are prepared to answer questions thoroughly and that their answers and descriptions align with yours. Just like several other aspects of leading this change, this will take some time, but it will be well worth it.

4. See the qualifications for elders and deacons in 1 Tim 3.

5. Keep in mind that they will be helping lead the congregation to understand this new polity; therefore, the team should include some of the most knowledgeable individuals in your church regarding an elder polity. If you choose someone who helps fill in your blind spots, has a high Christian character, and is respected by the body but lacks understanding of the subject at hand, then you have not made a good selection. For this reason, I recommend only selecting individuals who attend the training, seminars, or sermons you offer on this subject.

Even if the members have already gone through your church-wide, broader training, they will likely benefit from a revised version. The first couple of meetings should be a deeper study than what you offered to the entire congregation. Consider asking the team about areas where they lack understanding and spend extra time on them. I also recommend asking one or two of them to lead portions of the review; most of us learn more thoroughly when we prepare to teach. You can also offer them podcasts, books, or articles about elder polity to discuss. Whatever you can do to help them feel more knowledgeable and prepared will be time well spent.

Once you feel the team is adequately prepared to answer questions, begin using them as part of the process of leading the change. Ensure they understand that they have a perspective that you don't, and each of them has been strategically chosen to help guide this process. Give them the freedom to challenge assumptions you make or ideas you propose. Then, ask them questions like "What is something you feel is unclear about the material we are sharing with the congregation?" or "What is a question you have, or have heard, about this process that I didn't answer in the church-wide sessions?" When they give you feedback, make sure to receive it well, rather than defensively. If you have chosen the team correctly, then you know they are part of this process to help and not hurt. Thank them for offering the feedback, and do your best to address their questions or implement changes based on their concerns.

You also need to ensure that the congregation is aware of the lead team, its role, and its members. Publish their names on any handouts you create for this process, have the team on stage with you during Q&A times, allow them opportunities to share why they are in favor of this change, and recommend that church members seek guidance directly from team members and not just from you. This level of transparency breeds confidence that you aren't doing this alone, and you aren't the only one convinced it is useful.

PERSONAL EXPERIENCE

At Mt. Zion, we made every effort to ensure the congregation understood that the lead team was fully supportive of this change and an integral part of the process. We published their names on documents we created, had them stand on stage with me during updates about the process, put their names on the screens while making announcements, and I regularly recommended that church members sit down with the team members one-on-one to find answers to their questions. Additionally, if we decided to implement one of their ideas, I made sure to give them credit for it. This went even further in helping the church see that I was not the only one involved in leading this transition.

I believe one of the most meaningful ways we utilized the lead team was during one of our "town hall meetings." This was a designated time when I was going to address questions that had arisen and present some new documents to the congregation. During this particular meeting, I asked each team member to take three to five minutes to share their reasons for supporting the proposed change. Their answers varied greatly. One of the ladies shared in a profoundly emotional way about a nephew of hers who was serving in a church with this polity and the difference it had made in his life. She became overwhelmed and even cried while sharing. Another brother shared that "his mama had always told them that two heads were better than one, even if one was a goat!"[6] The vast difference in their reasons for supporting the change resonated deeply with the congregation, and I believe it significantly influenced many members who

6. I almost named this book *Two Heads Are Better Than One, Even If One Is a Goat*. However, you probably wouldn't be reading it right now if I would have!

were unsure simply from hearing me discuss the newly proposed polity.

A lead team is an important resource that I cannot recommend highly enough. There is a lot of work that goes into properly selecting, training, and deploying one, but the benefits are almost irreplaceable. To gain such a vast amount of the congregation's trust and influence by surrounding yourself with wise and Christlike people is a no-brainer.

A wisely chosen and properly trained lead team will have a significant influence on you and the congregation. However, we don't want to limit the influence used in this process to those whom we find locally. There is also a way to leverage the influence of Christians from outside the current congregation. This is where we will turn our attention now, as we consider the power of trusted testimonies.

THE INFLUENCE OF OTHERS—UTILIZING TRUSTED TESTIMONIES

I recently bought a pair of replacement lenses for my sunglasses. I didn't want to spend the money to purchase them directly from the original manufacturer, but I was somewhat overwhelmed by the number of aftermarket lenses available. Some cost more, some less, some had better warranties, while others had none at all, and none of them were brands with which I had any experience. What ultimately made the difference in the lenses I chose? A personal recommendation from a trusted friend.

I remembered one day when my associate pastor and I were riding to town with our minister of music, and he picked up his sunglasses and said, "Check out the lenses in these, I got them from _______ (aftermarket lens company)." He then went on to discuss their quality and reasonable prices. A few months later, when I needed new lenses, I remembered that conversation, asked him which company it was, and decided to purchase from them.

In the world of marketing, this is referred to as word-of-mouth marketing (WOM). A 2024 article from Investopedia defines WOM as what happens "when consumers talk about a company's product or service to their friends, family, and others with whom they have close relationships."[7] One of the most remarkable aspects of WOM is its effectiveness. In the article, the author says, "WOM marketing is one of the most powerful forms of advertising as 88% of consumers trust their friends' recommendations over traditional media."[8]

None of this should be new or surprising to us. I already gave the example of choosing where I would buy my lenses based on Shane's recommendation, and I'm sure you all have examples as well. Companies often go to great lengths to encourage people to provide testimonials or reviews of their products, and we can utilize this approach when leading a change in polity, too. We've already utilized WOM to an extent by utilizing a lead team. Let's consider another way we can utilize WOM in the process of leading this change.

Using Trusted Testimonies When Shifting Polity

It seems that your choice of who you can get to share a testimony about this polity is limited to the members currently in the church. It isn't very practical to think that another pastor can come on a Sunday morning or Wednesday night, just to talk about polity. It's also not very feasible for someone living a couple of states away to join the discussion. However, we live in an age of media. Emails, recorded videos, and even Zoom meetings are as easy to obtain as in-person testimonies. You can gather some of these from trusted

7. Hayes, "Word-of-Mouth Marketing," para. 1.

8. This statistic is based on a 2021 study by Nielsen titled "Trust in Advertising" that included individuals from over 56 countries. Hayes, "Word-of-Mouth Marketing," para. 7.

individuals and incorporate them into your teaching series or town hall meetings.

The first step in this process is to consider individuals who have previously been part of your church family, or are closely connected to it, and who can speak personally and favorably about a plural elder polity. Here are some categories to think through:

- Are there any young men or women who grew up in the church who have gone on to become members or leaders in a church with a plural elder polity?
- Are there any previous pastors or staff members who are currently serving in a church that employs a plural elder polity?
- Is there a local associational director or someone from your state convention whom the church knows well and trusts who is an advocate of plural elder polity?
- Are there any previous interim pastors who fit this category?
- Is there an author or denominational leader whom your church particularly trusts and admires who is an advocate for a plural elder polity?

Once you compile a database of individuals, prayerfully consider whom you want to contact. First, express gratitude for the godly influence they have exhibited in your current church. Then, explain what you aim to do in leading this change in polity. Last, ask if they would be willing to send a personal letter of recommendation that you could read to the church, or even better, if they would record a brief (two to five minute) video explaining why they would recommend your church consider adopting this polity.

Consider asking them to highlight the differences they have personally experienced between a single-pastor church and one with a plural elder polity. Such personal recommendations are often received much like a friend suggesting you try a new restaurant. For any members who might be uncertain, these personal videos or letters can offer clarity and assurance.

After you receive the letters or videos, look for ways to incorporate them into the education process. Show the videos at the end of a church service, or use them in your curriculum. Publish the individual letters in your church bulletin or other communication (weekly emails, social media). Ensure that they are visible to as many people as possible, as WOM marketing is only effective when it is heard/seen.

Seeking these testimonies from trusted individuals allows you to further grow the confidence of the congregation. It is one thing if their Sunday school teacher or chairman of deacons is an advocate of this shift in polity. However, it is quite another if a former pastor, deacon, or member, now immersed in a church with an elder polity, is able to compare and contrast the two and end by personally recommending this shift.

PERSONAL EXPERIENCE

Mt. Zion was particularly gifted in this area, as several young men and women who grew up or served here have gone on to be part of churches with a plural elder polity. Several young men who were raised in this church and community went with Tony Merida to plant Imago Dei in North Carolina. Several of them were not only part of the plant team but also went on to serve as elders in that church. Two other young men served as elders at Immanuel Community Church in New Orleans. All of these young men still have family members at Mt. Zion, and therefore, we still see them from time to time.

What a gift to realize that MZBC had a good handful of young men who grew up here, who had gone on to serve as elders/pastors in churches with a plural elder polity! These men had the trust of the congregation due to their long-term relationship, and they had personally seen the differences between a single-pastor polity and a plural elder one. These young men were strong advocates for this change, still have family at MZBC, and periodically come back to visit with us.[9] These young men checked both boxes; they were trusted friends, and they could personally attest to the greater health found in a plural elder polity.

I already had a relationship with these young men, so I reached out to them to ask if they would be willing to write a letter or record a video. Thankfully, I received multiple letters and videos, which I was able to incorporate into the teaching sessions. I believe this made a significant difference in how the church viewed this potential transition.

As they read the letters or sat and watched the videos, what they saw were young men they had taught and helped raise, their friend's children, their former classmates and neighbors, men they respected, telling them about the difference this transition had made in their lives and the lives of their families and churches; this was powerful. MZBC members viewed these videos and read these letters as recommendations from trusted friends who had once sat in their seats and stood in their shoes. These were not only personal recommendations but also the testimonies of people who had already made this transition and had witnessed the blessings that came with it.

These brothers weren't simply recommending a theoretical idea they had heard of or read about. These men weren't actors in a commercial. No, these were real people sharing their own experiences.

They discussed the major differences they had noticed between these two models. How having multiple pastors/elders allowed the work to be done more fully, and the pastor to rest more completely. They talked about

9. I know not every church will be as blessed as MZBC when it comes to this. However, elder polity has become much more prevalent over the previous twenty years, and I trust there is someone in your association, state convention, denomination, at a local seminary, or who used to serve on staff who can serve as an advocate for this form of leadership.

the sustainability of the plural elder model, and they did so personally and emphatically!

This was truly word-of-mouth marketing at its best, and the measure of its effectiveness seemed to be off the charts. Based on the data presented from Nielsen, it is likely that a high percentage of MZBC members felt more positive about this decision after viewing the letters and videos.

Using these tools—a lead team and trusted testimonies—is another step in the leadership process. It is part of vision casting, but it is also part of leading well. It utilizes the influence of people the congregation loves to help foster greater confidence in them.

CONCLUSION

Influence is a real thing, and it is potent. We are all influenced by outside sources every day. We are influenced by celebrities and influencers, compelled by commercials, and even more thoroughly influenced by trusted friends and family. This powerful force can be used to coerce and manipulate, but it can also be used in proper and appropriate ways to help people see and be open to things they have not considered before. This is what we aim to achieve by leveraging the influence of others to help lead a change in polity.

We do not want to manipulate emotions or pressure people into doing something they don't want to do. We don't want to coerce or use other inappropriate tactics to compel members to make a decision they are uncomfortable with. Instead, we aim to draw on the personal experiences and convictions of trusted leaders and friends to provide clarity and confidence in a biblical pattern of church leadership.

Through the avenues recommended in this chapter, you can ensure you and others are influenced in a healthy and appropriate way.

When leading a change, there will always be things you miss; you won't see every possible perspective. However, when you employ a wise and diverse team of individuals to help you—a lead team—you ensure more of those perspectives are seen and heard. Take the time to consider your deficiencies, select people who can help fill those gaps, and offer them a strong voice in leading this change.

Through the lead team, you also gain the trust and influence that team members have earned. It's as if you take the collective trust and confidence the church has in them and add it to the trust and confidence they have in you!

However, when you put them on the lead team, you are offering them a position of influence and leadership. By providing them a seat next to you on the platform, you are telling the church they are trustworthy brothers and sisters. Therefore, it is crucial that you not only select well-known and influential members but also individuals of high Christian character.

A properly chosen lead team is a powerful tool when leading congregational change. It enables you to tap into the influence of some of the strongest, most well-known, and influential members to foster confidence in this change. However, you don't want to limit the influence of spiritually mature and thoroughly convinced Christians to current church members, and that's where the use of trusted testimonies comes in.

When you reach out to former members or denominational leaders to provide videos and letters advocating for this change, you are harnessing the influence of these leaders to instill even more confidence and excitement in church members. Our current digital age allows you to easily access men and women all over the world, and it also allows them to share their convictions and experiences with the church. These testimonies can be powerful and offer confidence to those who might still be somewhat uncertain about this change.

When you pair the local influence of a lead team with the far-reaching impact of other trusted leaders, you have a comprehensive plan for employing word-of-mouth marketing to help lead a change in polity.

At this point, you have determined the proper timing and combined it with biblical teaching, practical application, and the comprehensive influence of godly people both inside and outside the church. You have now completed the education and vision-casting phases of leading the change.

You are now ready to begin the actual transition. As you consider implementing this new polity, there are still tasks to be completed and necessary steps to be taken. The next chapter addresses many of these steps.

6

Making It Happen

Necessary Steps to Complete the Transition

A MIXTURE OF NERVES and confidence, that's how I would describe my feelings on the morning of my first (and only) marathon.

The reasons why it was my only marathon are for another day, but I would like to take a moment to discuss the reason there were nerves and confidence in the same package—a feeling many of you likely share if you have come this far in the process of preparing a church to change its polity.

I felt confident because I had undergone a rigorous training program that lasted months. Prior to the race, I followed a detailed, five-month training plan. Knowing you have completed all the necessary steps to prepare for something gives you a great deal of confidence.

However, I still had a small amount of nerves. Why, why would someone who had prepared so vigorously still feel nervous? Well, despite having prepared well, I still had to run 26.2 miles!

Similarly, you have done a lot of preparation, but the final steps can still seem quite scary. By this point, you should share that feeling of confidence. You have spent a considerable amount of time researching your church's history and having individual discussions. You have also completed teaching sessions or a sermon series. You've selected, trained, and employed a lead team. You've utilized handouts and prayed for hours.

Take a moment to acknowledge the effort you have put into this, and let that realization give you the confidence that you and the church are prepared to take the next step.

Nevertheless, you probably still feel a certain amount of nervousness also. Though you have laid the groundwork and prepared well, you still need to take the final steps to implement this new leadership model.

This chapter is designed to be a nuts-and-bolts description of the necessary steps to bring this change in polity to completion. It is broken down into two categories: (a) steps for making the transition official, and (b) steps for implementing the new polity.

Let's begin by examining the parliamentary procedures and legal requirements that must be fulfilled before implementing the new polity.

STEPS FOR MAKING THE TRANSITION OFFICIAL

There are only a few simple steps remaining to make the transition official (legally speaking). These should be undertaken before beginning the process of implementing the polity, so we will look at them first.

Before we proceed to the actual changes, I would like to provide a disclaimer: you must consult your bylaws or governing documents to determine precisely what's necessary to make this change in your local church. Each church has peculiarities in its bylaws and processes, and I'm not familiar with yours. I will speak from a ten-thousand-foot perspective here. Any specifics given will be taken from Robert's Rules of Order (RONR).

There Must Be an Official Vote

The first step to make the change official is to hold a vote. If you are in a congregationally governed church (like Mt. Zion and most Southern Baptist churches), then this vote will need to be a church-wide vote in a business or members meeting. If your church's bylaws specify a different process, follow that one.[1]

Now that we know that a vote is required, let's consider points of order that should be taken into account. Understanding the requirements of this type of vote will ensure everything is handled appropriately.

Specifics of the Vote

Because this is categorized as an "Amendment of Bylaws"[2] vote, it requires a couple of things to pass. First, this type of vote requires prior notice.[3] For most churches, this will require an announcement to be made at least two weeks in advance. Therefore, this type of vote requires prior planning.

The second requirement for this type of vote is a two-thirds majority. This means at least two-thirds of those present and voting must vote in favor of the change.[4] Also, since a vote requiring

1. It is likely that some churches will require a vote by the deacons, staff, or personnel committee before taking a vote to the entire congregation. Others might only require a vote by the pastor and deacons and not the congregation as a whole. Again, consult your bylaws.

2. Details about an "Amendment of Bylaws" motion are found in section 57 of the twelfth edition of *Robert's Rules of Order*. Robert et al., *Robert's Rules*, 560.

3. The church likely has a precedent for what "prior notice" means, but if it doesn't, you can refer to the definition from *Robert's Rules of Order* in section 10:44 of the twelfth edition. In short, it means that when you announce the meeting, you specifically announce that this particular motion will be part of the meeting. Robert et al., *Robert's Rules*, 112.

4. This is a very specific definition. According to RONR, blanks or abstentions are not counted in this vote. Therefore, you only need two-thirds of the votes cast. Robert et al., *Robert's Rules*, 560.

a two-thirds majority must be counted accurately, this type of vote should not be taken as a voice vote.[5]

Those details are important for parliamentary procedure and ensuring that everything seems to have been done "above board" and with full transparency. Another important aspect of parliamentary procedure is the framing of the actual motion. Let's briefly consider that.

Specifics of the Motion

It is essential to be precise with your language when drafting this motion. It should ensure nothing is unclear or seemingly improper about the process. Imagine you are a church member reading back through the church's minutes fifty years from now. You should be able to understand precisely what was being voted on without much interpretation.[6]

After completing the months (or years) of research and education, formulating the motion, and making the necessary prior announcement, it is finally time to vote on this change!

PERSONAL EXPERIENCE

At Mt. Zion, we announced the motion two weeks in advance of the vote and encouraged any members who still had questions to speak with me or a member of the lead team. We held the vote at the end of a Sunday morning service to ensure that as many members as possible were present. At the conclusion of the service, we dismissed all guests and officially entered into a business meeting. We

5. Robert et al., *Robert's Rules*, 404–6. The standard way to hold this type of vote is by standing, but in a smaller assembly, it can be done by a show of hands, and if a motion is made for it to be by ballot, that is allowable as well.

6. I have included the actual motion used at Mt. Zion in the "Personal Experience Section" below.

decided to follow the standard recommendation of holding a standing vote on the matter.[7]

I presented the official motion, which read,

> "I move that Mt. Zion Baptist Church adopt a plural pastor polity that includes both staff and non-staff pastors. We authorize the nominating committee to recommend a pastoral assessment committee to identify and assess potential non-staff pastors. The church's bylaws and governing documents shall be amended as necessary to reflect this change in polity."[8]

Here are the key points that we deemed necessary to address in the motion:

- The first thing we wanted to clarify was that our new structure would encompass both staff and non-staff (or lay) pastors. We already had the allowance of multiple staff pastors (associate pastors, youth pastors, etc.), but the significant change for us was the allowance of non-staff pastors. We felt adding "that includes both staff and non-staff pastors" helped define what we meant by "plural pastor polity."
- The second central point we wanted to address was the process for beginning to affirm non-staff pastors. We already had a process in place for hiring staff pastors, but seeking, finding, and affirming non-staff pastors was a new endeavor. Therefore, we empowered the nominating committee to recommend a pastoral

7. Meaning we literally had all those in favor stand, and after they were counted and seated, we asked all those opposed to stand and counted them.

8. At MZBC we opted to use the term "plural pastoral polity" instead of elder polity. Since we believe these two terms (pastor and elder) are synonyms, and the term "pastor" is much more familiar at Mt. Zion, we decided to stick with it. You could substitute "elder polity" or "plural elder polity" in its place. Whatever term you use, make sure it is clear to the body what it means. For an explanation of the pastoral assessment committee, continue reading this chapter.

assessment committee (PAC, more on them later in this chapter) to the church. The work of this new committee is outlined in our policies and procedures, where all committee descriptions can be found.

- The final point we wanted to address was the amending of the governing documents. At Mt. Zion, this change required amending language and descriptions in our bylaws and policies and procedures manual. We did not want to get bogged down by these specifics during this business meeting, so we acknowledged the changes and presented them to the church for final approval at a later time.

The church voted in favor of this change, and it became the official polity of Mt. Zion on April 30, 2023. The final count was 95 percent in favor, with 5 percent against. Then, it was time to implement this change.

Ensuring the vote is properly passed might feel like the finish line, but it is not. It is an exciting moment, and one you should celebrate! However, after the vote is passed, there is still much work to be done. The next section is dedicated to helping you consider how to turn your shared vision into a realized reality!

STEPS FOR IMPLEMENTING THE NEW POLITY

Once the church agrees to adopt this new leadership structure, you will need a process for identifying, assessing, and presenting potential elders to the body. In this section, I will offer popular methods for each of these tasks.

Identifying Candidates

One of the first things you need to decide is how to identify candidates. Two of the most common methods for doing this are (1) allowing the congregation to make nominations, or (2) having a specific group make nominations.

When allowing the congregation to make nominations, the church could opt for an open nomination process where any member can nominate a potential elder at any time, or they can set a specific time period during which nominations are accepted.[9] One of the greatest strengths of this method is that it ensures every member has the opportunity to nominate potential elders. One of the greatest weaknesses is that it allows nominations without requiring a thorough assessment of each candidate.[10]

When the church chooses to have a specific group handle the task of identifying candidates, it has the advantage of ensuring the candidates are thoroughly vetted and assessed before being presented. The group chosen should be tasked with presenting only candidates who meet the biblical requirements to serve in the office.

When a church chooses this method, they have multiple options. They can adopt the elder-only approach, the committee approach, or a hybrid approach. Let's briefly consider each.

Elders Only Approach

Some churches adopt the view that potential elders should only be identified, assessed, and nominated by other elders. In this approach, the elders exclusively fulfill this task. One of the greatest strengths of this is how thoroughly candidates are assessed. They

9. This time period can be whatever the church chooses. It could all be done in a single business meeting, or nominations could be accepted for an entire month or more.

10. In a congregational nomination, there is always the potential that men are recommended based on popularity or other unbiblical qualifications. I highly recommend that nominees be thoroughly vetted by someone or some group before being presented to the church for a formal vote. This can save a lot of embarrassment and heartache.

are being vetted by elders, men who have served in this office and know the requirements well. In the long run, this option can be very beneficial to the body.

One of the greatest weaknesses of this approach is that it requires the first generation of plural elders to be identified, assessed, and recommended by one man alone. Since the church currently only has one elder (the senior pastor), he is required to undertake this task by himself, and that is a heavy burden.

Committee Approach

Another popular option is to use a committee approach. In this approach, the church elects or appoints a select group of individuals to identify, assess, and recommend potential lay elders to the body. In some churches, this group will simply be an already established group or committee (deacons, Personnel Committee, Nominating Committee, or other) or a subcommittee chosen from one of these standing groups. However, other churches opt to appoint or elect a brand-new committee, just like they would a pastor search committee.

One of the greatest strengths of this approach is that it allows the task to be fulfilled by a select group who can be trained and prepared for the task, and it never requires just one man to do it alone. Another strength is that this approach allows a church to incorporate women into the identification, assessment, and nomination process without requiring that it be open to the entire congregation.

One of the greatest weaknesses of this approach is that it means that the process will be fulfilled by men and/or women who have never served as elders. They don't understand the unique challenges of the office, which can result in a less thorough identification and assessment process.

Hybrid Approach

I am aware of one church that employed a hybrid model, where a committee conducted the initial identification, assessment, and nomination process, but all future iterations were handled exclusively by the elders.

In this church, the first batch of elders (six) was identified, assessed, and nominated exclusively by a newly formed committee. After this group of men was elected and officially became elders, the committee was dissolved, and the elder board took over the process of identifying, assessing, and presenting all future candidates.

Obviously, this approach allows the strengths of the previous two approaches to be combined. No man is ever tasked with doing this alone, and the majority of the assessments are handled exclusively by elders.

However, it does require that the first set of elders be chosen by non-elder members, and it also requires a good bit of work (choosing the committee, training the committee) for only a short period of active service.

PERSONAL EXPERIENCE

At Mt. Zion, we opted for a different hybrid approach. From the outside looking in, it appears that we chose the committee approach. We did elect a new committee to serve in the identification, assessment, and nomination process; we call them the Pastoral Assessment Committee (PAC). The PAC is comprised of three men and two women. However, all elders are automatically members of the PAC as well. That means, currently, our PAC consists of eight individuals, three men and two women elected by the congregation, along with our three pastors.

It was important to us to have men and women, as well as pastors and non-pastors, serving as part of this process. This goes back to the discussion about blind spots from chapter five. The biggest question we received was about having women on the PAC, but we felt it was important.[11] In addition to the perspective women bring to the PAC, the committee also interviews the candidate's wife (if married) and other family members, sometimes including daughters, during the assessment process. We have found that these conversations are often enhanced by having female committee members.

Another reason we chose the committee-based approach and included men and women on it is that this is the precedent set at Mt. Zion. When electing search committees to identify staff pastors, the church has always relied on committees made up of men and women. We would have needed a compelling reason to break this pattern, but we found none. Therefore, we decided the process that had worked well in identifying and assessing potential staff pastors for decades would work well for identifying and assessing lay pastors.

Obviously, each of the approaches found in this section has strengths and weaknesses that need to be considered, and each church is free to choose the approach that works best for them. After the vote has been secured and the identification and assessment approach is agreed upon, there are only a few final details to be considered before electing your first lay elder. I will address several of those in the following section.

11. A hypothetical scenario we considered involves a man who appears to be a great candidate to other men. He is knowledgeable, doctrinally sound, and theologically astute. However, there are times when astute men like this interact with women in a way that makes them feel uncomfortable. I won't offer specific scenarios, but you can probably imagine what I'm talking about. If you had such a candidate in your church, you wouldn't want him to serve as pastor. This hypothetical situation helped us recognize the importance of having men and women on the PAC.

QUICK HITTERS

In this section, we will briefly consider several more minor decisions. For each, I will address the decision, offer possible choices, and explain what we did at Mt. Zion.

Presenting Individuals or Groups

Are the elders or committee you have chosen to identify, assess, and nominate candidates going to work with one man at a time, or will they bring a slate of nominees all at once?

A strength of the individual approach is that the assessment can be more thorough. The assessing group is not required to consider multiple men simultaneously, which can lead to comparison or cutting corners. Instead, they have one candidate whom they consider thoroughly, present to the congregation for a vote, and then move on to another candidate.

One weakness of this approach is that the church is only able to add one elder at a time. If the church needs to add four or five elders, this process can be lengthy.

The group approach has the opposite effect. A strength is that you can add multiple candidates (three, four, five, etc.) at one time. The weakness is that the committee and the congregation usually end up looking at the overall slate more and each candidate less.

PERSONAL EXPERIENCE

MZBC decided to present candidates one at a time. This has made the process slower, but it has also allowed it to be more deliberate. When we weighed the two, deliberation was more valuable to us than expediency.

Number of Elders

Some churches that adopt this polity have as few as two elders, while others have double-digit elders. Scripture does not prescribe a specific number of elders for each church, nor is there a universally accepted ratio. Two of the main factors here will be (a) the size of the congregation, and (b) the number of qualified men the church has?[12]

PERSONAL EXPERIENCE

MZBC decided not to set a specific number of elders. We have no minimum (other than our desire to maintain at least two) and no maximum. We aim to maintain a 1:1 ratio of staff to lay elders, and we are working towards achieving this goal. At the moment, we have two staff elders and one lay, but we thank the Lord that we currently have other men who are considering taking the next step.

How to Present Candidates

Once you have decided on the number and identified and assessed one or more candidates, you need to determine how to present them to the body. Some churches opt for a lengthier process because the men are local and available. Still, others decide to stick with the standard procedure for presenting a new senior pastor (typically a one- or two-day event). Here are a few options to consider for this presentation process:

12. One of the most frequently asked questions I receive from pastors of small churches is, "What do I do if I don't have any men who meet the qualifications to serve as a pastor?" My answer is always the same: pray and begin discipling some.

- How long do you want to set aside for prayer and consideration from the day the candidate is announced before the actual vote?
- Do you want to make the candidate available for a question-and-answer session?
- Do you want the candidate to share their testimony before the body?
- Do you want the candidate to preach or teach before the body?
- Do your guiding documents require a certain procedure for adding new pastors/elders?
- How long do you want to allow between each step in the process?

Answering these questions will help you determine how long the process should be and precisely what it will look like. Once you decide how many steps are necessary and how long you should allow between each step, you have a timeline for presenting the candidate.

PERSONAL EXPERIENCE

At Mt. Zion, we opted for a four-week minimum process. We give members a whole month to consider candidates, and have some public presentations during our Sunday morning service each week during that period. On the first Sunday, we announce the candidate and have a prayer for them. On the second Sunday, the candidate shares his testimony and explains why he feels called to the office. On the third Sunday, the candidate either teaches a joint Sunday school class for all adults (in our sanctuary) or preaches during the morning service.[13] On the fourth and final Sunday, we hold the official vote.

13. This is to demonstrate that he meets the qualification of "able to teach" from 1 Tim 3:2. It does not specify being able to preach, so we allow the candidate to choose which option he feels more suited to do.

Details for the Documents

We already know that it is necessary to amend your governing documents to implement this new leadership structure, but several factors need to be considered when doing so. You will want to include the minimum and maximum number of elders, any staff-to-elder ratios, and the transition process in the governing documents.[14]

However, you might also want to include details like these:

- Will there be a rotational basis for elders?
- If so, how long will elder terms last?
- If so, how long must a man sit out from serving after his first term before he is eligible to begin a new term?
- Who will be the head of the elder board (elected, appointed, or simply the senior pastor)?
- How will elders be removed if they become disqualified?
- What percentage of votes is required to call/confirm an elder candidate (simple majority, two-thirds, 75 percent, etc.)
- If the church is without any staff pastors (an interim period), will the elders still rotate or remain active through the interim process?
- Will all staff pastors serve as elders or only the senior pastor?[15]

These details will serve as guidelines, enabling the church to have a clearer vision for what this process will look like. Let's face it, there will be a day when you aren't pastor of that church

14. Some churches might opt to put several of these "operational details" in their policies and procedures manual rather than in their bylaws.

15. This is likely not a concern for smaller churches but is one to be considered for larger churches with multiple staff pastors. I am personally an advocate for having all staff pastors serve as elders. If we say the terms pastor and elder are synonyms (and they are in Scripture), then I don't understand why a pastor would not serve on the elder board. However, there are healthy churches I greatly respect who follow this pattern. You must decide for your church.

any longer. These particulars will allow this polity to continue and flourish even in your absence.

PERSONAL EXPERIENCE

At Mt. Zion, we have taken all these matters into account. We expanded the "Pastor" section of our bylaws considerably. For one, we wanted to be thorough, but I also know that some of our leaders had concerns about what they would do when I am no longer here to guide this process. Taking the time to consider as many details as possible felt like a tangible and appropriate way for me to shepherd the body.

To assist with this process, I contacted multiple churches that had already made this transition and requested copies of their guiding documents. This was an excellent tool that revealed several things we had not considered yet. It also provided us with a clear picture of how to document these operational details. If you know of churches that are a little ahead of you in this process, consider contacting them and requesting a copy of their guiding documents. In my experience, they were all more than happy to help in this way.[16]

I know there are many details in this chapter. It's unlikely you have taken them all in fully, and that's okay. My prayer is that this chapter will serve as a valuable resource you can return to when needed. However, I would like to conclude with some encouragement for you.

16. If you need to, feel free to reach out to me or the leadership of Mt. Zion, and we will gladly share our documents.

CONCLUSION

Friends, you are so close to the finish line! You have already run a significant portion of the race. You have done the work, and now you are at the implementation phase. Don't stop now!

These details might seem like "fine print" or "unnecessary," but they are not. Remember, you aren't just changing the polity of a church; you are establishing a biblical pattern of pastoral ministry that will benefit the church and kingdom for years to come.

Every detail matters now, and as time passes, they will matter more. Currently, these details matter because they create confidence in the congregation. They show that you have thoroughly prepared and considered every aspect of this transition.

They will matter even more in the future because one day, the church you are serving will have a different senior pastor, and he might not be as knowledgeable as you on the subject. On that day, there will be questions you won't be around to answer. Providing clearly defined plans and guiding documents is a loving way to shepherd the church now and in the future.

The biblical pattern of plural elder polity will continue to serve God's people long after you are gone, so ensure the foundation it is built upon is solid.

Let me end by encouraging you not to lose sight of the finish line. You have endured a great deal, and the Lord has shown you much favor. Now is not the time to stop and rest but to push on towards the end. Trust me, you will be thankful you did!

7

Begin the Work

From Reading to Leading

When running a race, it is one thing to see the finish line, but it is quite another to cross it! When the finish line is finally in sight, you know you are close; you can feel all the hard work you have done finally paying off. Your legs ache and lungs burn, but your preparation is adequate to carry you through to the end.

Pastor or leader, you desire to cross the finish line of leading a change in polity. You want to successfully lead a church to adopt a plural elder polity, and now you know it is achievable, even in your current context. However, there is work to be done before you get there.

NEXT STEPS

What are those necessary steps? Let's review the recommended steps from this book, and I'll offer a realistic timeline for when to begin and complete each one:

- Assessment
    - Begin now, complete in one to six months

You should start having conversations with staff and key leaders now. You should also begin reviewing historical and guiding documents, as well as assessing the effectiveness and tenure of your leadership at the church. This research will enable you to properly assess the church's readiness to begin discussing this change.

Look back at the indicators from chapter 1 to use as guideposts. The questions you need to ask and the factors you need to consider are also found there.

Don't jump the gun on the process. Let the feedback and answers you receive guide you to a realistic timeline for implementing this change.

- Education
    - Begin at the proper time, complete over two to eighteen months

The education process encompasses all the information presented in chapters 2 and 3. This phase should include helping the church recognize that the current polity is inadequate in multiple ways, highlighting the biblical pattern of plural elder leadership, and explaining the benefits this new polity will afford. There is no specific pattern required for this teaching (e.g., Wednesday night, Sunday morning, class, sermon series); the most important thing is that the information is accurately conveyed.

Take your time in teaching this; the education phase is one of the most crucial. Be open and vulnerable when necessary. If this phase is properly presented, then the body should begin to desire this new form of leadership.

- Vision Casting
    - Begin after the education phase, complete over three to nine months

The vision-casting process is covered in chapter 4. This phase will enable the congregation to grasp the concept of having multiple pastors/elders and envision how it would be implemented in local practice. This is like putting flesh on a skeleton.

Many members will struggle to visualize this polity in practice. They haven't read about it, listened to pastors talk about it, or seen it implemented in another church. Therefore, it is important that you utilize visual aids, question-and-answer sessions, and handouts to provide them with a more comprehensive understanding of this polity in practice.

- Utilize Influence
  - Begin simultaneously with vision casting, complete over three to six months

The process of utilizing current members and influential Christians outside of the body to help build greater confidence is covered in chapter 5. The first step in this process is to build a lead team.

This lead team will be used during the vision casting phase more to help influence you. They will help ensure your blind spots are covered and you answer all the church's questions.

However, they will eventually be used in conjunction with the trusted testimony of outside voices to help the congregation feel more confident about this transition process.

- Implementation
  - Begin when the congregation is ready to vote, complete over one to eighteen months
    - Vote: one month
    - Identification and assessment: three to six months
    - Presentation and confirmation: one to three months

This phase is a lengthy one[1] because it begins with the parliamentary procedures necessary to make this change official and

1. I recognize that the ranges offered in this chapter are vast. However, if you refer to previous chapters—specifically to chapter 1—you will find more clear guidance. I offer these as sobering and realistic expectations. For some churches, this shift will be done a year from now. For some, it will be several years. I don't want to sugarcoat this fact.

stretches all the way through assessing and presenting candidates to serve as lay elders. This information is covered in chapter 6.

There are numerous details in this phase, but they are crucial for the short-term success of this transition and for the long-term health of the church.

Each phase in this process is valuable in its own way. Take your time and follow the progression from beginning to end. This preparation and training will enable you to eventually cross the finish line.

Let me share an overview of the results of all this work at Mt. Zion.

PERSONAL EXPERIENCE

At Mt. Zion, we have been so blessed by this transition. It has proven to be all I expected and more. This structure is still relatively new to us—at the time of writing, we have officially had this model in place for about two years. We are still finalizing a few details, but there will always be minor adjustments to make.

While some of the final details are still in the works, the blessing of serving in a plurality of elders is in full swing! Remember, I am at a church that is closer in size to most Southern Baptist churches. We are not a mega church, not by a long shot. Our average attendance is around 250. Currently, we only have one lay elder and two staff elders. However, even with only one lay elder added, the difference is tremendous!

Consider it from a ratio perspective: we've added 33 percent more pastoral coverage than we had before! Having the extra hands, additional wisdom, new giftings, and added perspective has been invaluable.

Don (our current lay elder) is over twenty years my senior and has been a church member for decades. He brings a great deal of wisdom and perspective to our elder board, for which I am grateful.

Not only has the addition of this one lay elder been a huge blessing but the transition to a plural elder polity has also shifted the church's view of our associate pastor. Traditionally, the church has seen this role as being a "junior pastor" or "pastor in training."

However, shifting our mindset to recognize that God has empowered churches to have multiple pastors (elders) has led the body to count Adam as a pastor as well. Practically speaking, through this transition, it is as if Mt. Zion has gained two new elders!

We praise God for allowing us to make this transition smoothly and joyfully.

ENDURING RESISTANCE

One thing that is almost inevitable is that you will face resistance. There will be people who speak against this transition both to you and to others. There will probably be at least a few members who will even lobby against it. Let me share a couple of thoughts on how to endure this resistance without being deterred.

Not Everyone Against the Change Is Against You

This is often hard for us to grasp or remember. Some people who will oppose this change love you, trust you, and are thankful for you. However, they simply don't want the church to make this change. These are likely the ones who will be open and honest with you about their concerns, and this is okay.

It is okay for God's people to disagree. We are called to unity but not always to single-mindedness. If they believe a different leadership structure would be better but make that known in humility and honesty, then they are well within their rights.

It will likely feel as though everyone opposed to this change is attacking you, but that simply is not true. Let this reminder help you continue on while still loving these brothers and sisters.

Opposition Is Part of Life in a Fallen World

We all know Jesus faced great persecution, as did the apostles after him. I believe Satan opposes healthy churches, and he will likely try to use different means to oppose this transition.

In leadership, you should expect opposition and have the courage to persevere through it undeterred. Will it be fun? No. Will you enjoy it? No. But can you get past it? Yes.

Prepare yourself in advance, trust in the Lord, surround yourself with mature believers, and continue to press on, even in the face of the attacks that are sure to come.

Lastly, I would like to encourage you to get after it!

CONCLUSION

God's desire is that his people become more and more sanctified until the point of glorification. He does this work through many means, but one of them is pastoral leadership.

Ephesians 4 makes it very clear that when this work is neglected, the consequences are dire. God has called pastors to ensure that Christians are shepherded, taught, mentored, equipped, and made more like Christ. The single pastor model has proven insufficient for this task in many of our churches. They need another model, one that allows for pastoral leadership to be comprehensively offered to every member—a plural elder model.

Therefore, remember that the work you are doing here is not unimportant or without consequence. It is valuable work that honors God and helps sanctify his people. Let this reminder help push you past the fear of what might happen if you take that first step.

Let it also carry us through the difficult times of resistance that will certainly come.

The work before you is worthwhile, and you are now prepared to begin it. So, go, and lead well for the glory of God and the good of his saints!

Appendix A

FAQ About Plural Pastoral Polity[1]

1. What is polity?

   Merriam-Webster defines it as "the form of government of a religious denomination."[2]

   It refers to the leadership structure of a church or organization.

2. What is a *plural pastoral polity*?

   It refers to having multiple men serving as pastors in one church.

   These men share pastoral leadership's tasks, duties, authority, and responsibilities. This is often accomplished by having a mixture of staff (paid) pastors and non-staff (unpaid) pastors.

   This is an alternative to a single pastor polity or a polity where a church has only one man serving as pastor.

3. Where does this idea come from?

   The idea is first found in the pages of the New Testament and is also well attested to throughout the history of the Christian church.

1. this is a document we distributed to the members of Mt. Zion during the education and vision casting phases of our transition

2. *Merriam-Webster*, "Polity."

In the book *40 Questions About Elders and Deacons*, Benjamin Merkle says this:

> The New Testament evidence indicates that every church had a plurality of elders. There is no example in the New Testament of one elder or pastor leading a congregation as the sole or primary leader.
>
> There were a plurality of elders at the churches in Jerusalem (Acts 11:30), Antioch of Pisidia, Lystra, Iconium, and Derbe (Acts 14:23), Ephesus (Acts 20:17; 1 Timothy 5:17); Philippi (Philippians 1:1), the cities of Crete (Titus 1:5), the churches in the dispersion to which James wrote (James 5:14), the churches in the Roman provinces of Pontus, Galatia, Cappadocia, Asia, and Bithynia (1 Peter 5:1), and possibly the church(es) to which Hebrews was written (Hebrews 13:7, 17, 24).[3]

This view—that the churches in the NT had multiple pastors—is widely accepted by pastors, scholars, and theologians.

4. Is this idea Baptist?

Yes, it is.

This was a regular occurrence in Baptist churches for much of their history and still is in many churches today.

In the book *Baptist Foundations*, Mark Dever says, "It is indisputable that at the beginning of the twentieth century, Baptists either had or advocated elders (pastors) in local churches—and often a plurality of elders (pastors). They had done so for centuries."[4]

This polity has been advocated for throughout Southern Baptist history, including by W. B. Johnson, the first president of the Southern Baptist Convention.[5]

3. Merkle, *40 Questions*, 164.
4. Dever, *Baptist Foundations*, 238.
5. Dever, *Baptist Foundations*, 236.

5. Do we know of any other Southern Baptist churches that practice this form of polity?

   You likely do. Immanuel Community Church in New Orleans (where Matthew Delaughter serves) does, as does Imago Dei Church in North Carolina (where several young men from Mt. Zion serve). Morrison Heights, Colonial Heights, and FBC Brandon in the Jackson metro area have this form of polity, and many other churches throughout Mississippi and the Southern Baptist Convention.

6. Are we talking about hiring more staff members?

   Not as a direct result of this decision. As mentioned in question 2, this polity is often a mixture of staff and non-staff pastors. That means we would have men like Brother Zach serving alongside other members here that meet all of the qualifications to be a pastor.

   These men would serve in a voluntary role and would not be paid (monetarily) for their time and service.

7. Would non-staff pastors have to meet the same qualifications as a staff pastor, like Brother Tim, Brother Chris, or Brother Zach do?

   Yes, all Biblical qualifications listed in 1 Tim 3 and Titus 1 would also apply to them. A pastor is a pastor, paid or not.

8. If we chose to swap to this form of polity, would it diminish the authority of the church members?

   No.

   Just like Brother Zach is not the "ruler" of Mt. Zion now, the pastors would not become the "rulers" then.

   The pastors would lead, not rule. They would not obtain more authority than the Bible already gives to the pastor's office.

   The hierarchy of Mt. Zion would remain the same:
   Christ → Congregation → Pastoral Leadership

9. What would happen to deacons?

   They would continue to serve and lead, and, in some ways, their calling would be accentuated or highlighted.

The office of deacon is biblical, and deacon ministry is imperative for a church to be as healthy as it should be.

The deacons would continue to serve as deacons as described in Scripture (specifically Acts 6:1–6).

The pastors would be in charge of pastoral things (teaching, leading, oversight, vision/direction, doctrine, discipline, etc.), and the deacons would help serve alongside them where needed. They would continue to carry out the biblical calling of the office.

However, with multiple pastors, deacons would not be asked to fulfill pastoral roles, thus freeing them up to do their work unencumbered.

10. What would happen to committees if we adopt this polity?

    Nothing, this polity doesn't require any change in committee structure.

    Our committees would continue to guide and lead in their respective specialty areas, all under the overall leadership of Christ, the church, and the pastors.

11. What would the job of these non-staff pastors be? Would they be expected to do all that Brother Zach does?

    They would not be full-time employees of the church, so their roles would not be the same as those of Brother Zach or any other staff pastor.

    They would *not* be expected to keep office hours. Some would likely be men with full-time jobs.

    However, while the amount of time devoted to pastoring would be lessened, they would share the same biblical calling and office. They would help lead in areas of teaching, prayer, direction and vision casting (leading), discipline, equipping, and shepherding.

12. Would Brother Zach still be the lead/senior pastor?

    Yes, he would.

    As the only (current) pastor who will be a full-time employee and with the most training and experience, he would continue to serve as the lead/senior pastor tasked with helping guide the pastoral—and overall—ministry of the church.

Brother Zach would still do the vast majority of the preaching, give oversight to the church ministries, and continue to lead in the ways he has—only it would be done with more assistance, wisdom, and gifting as these men came alongside him.

13. Is it wrong or sinful NOT to adopt this form of polity?

No, that is not the argument that is being made.

My (Brother Zach) view is that this constitutes the form of church government advocated for and adopted by the apostles and other New Testament leaders—when men like Paul, Peter, and John planted churches. When Timothy, Titus, and Silas planted or directed churches, they employed this form of leadership (polity).

It is not a matter of what we "must do" but what we "could/should do" to bring about greater spiritual health at MZBC.

Appendix B

Potential Job Description for Non-Staff Pastors[1]

A. *Qualifications*: Pastors must meet the biblical requirements for the office as detailed in 1 Tim 3 and Titus 1.

B. *Areas of Required Focus*: All pastors share the same overarching calls. These can be summed up as follows:

   1. Shepherding (Acts 20:28; 1 Pet 5:2)
   2. Teaching (1 Tim 3:2; Acts 20:20, 21, 27; 2 Tim 4:2)
   3. Leading (managing, giving oversight) (Acts 20:28; 1 Tim 3:4–5, 5:17; Heb 13:17)
   4. Exemplifying (being examples of godly living) (1 Pet 5:3; Heb 13:17; 1 Tim 4:12)
   5. Equipping (Eph 4:11–12; 2 Tim 2:2)

   The amount of time a pastor spends on any particular area will depend on their individual gifting, but all pastors will be expected to serve in each and every area listed here.

1. This is another document we distributed to the members of Mt. Zion during the education and vision casting phases of our transition

C. *Specific Duties for All Pastors*:

1. Make every effort to attend all regular meetings of MZBC.
2. Meet with the other pastors twice monthly (first Sunday morning at 8:00, third Sunday evening at 5:30).
3. Meet with and oversee at least one committee or ministry of the church.
4. Regularly pray for church members and help fulfill the callings listed in section B.

MOCK JOB DESCRIPTIONS FOR INDIVIDUALS BASED ON THEIR GIFTINGS

D. *(Possible job description for "Jim," who is more gifted at counseling, hospitality, and one-on-one teaching)*

Jim will help lead primarily in congregational care. If a church member is dealing with a difficult issue (work problems, marriage issues, death of a loved one, difficult diagnosis), and Jim is available, he will respond by meeting with those individuals to listen, pray, and offer scriptural advice. He will provide a monthly report to the rest of the pastors about members needing extra prayer or attention at the pastors' meeting.

While Jim will lead in congregational care, this task will be shared among all the pastors as needed.

E. *(Possible job description for "Carl," who is more gifted at equipping and preaching)*

Carl will help lead primarily in teaching and training. He will preach once per quarter and be the first pastor asked to preach anytime Brother Zach is out. He will also train our Sunday School teachers annually and provide additional training for church members as needed. He will provide a monthly report to the rest of the pastors on completed or needed training at the pastors' meeting.

While Carl will lead in teaching and training, all pastors will share this task as needed. This will include others preaching at certain times instead of Carl or Brother Zach.

F. *(Possible job description for "Bart," who is more gifted in administration and leading)*

Bart will help lead primarily in oversight and management. He will regularly meet with the heads of committees and ministries to receive updates and offer feedback on the work that they are doing. He will provide a monthly report to the rest of the pastors, summarizing these updates at the pastors' meeting. This report will include celebrations, concerns, or recommendations from committees/ministries.

While Bart will lead in oversight and management, this task will be shared among all pastors as needed. This will include each pastor having at least one committee or area of ministry that they oversee and meet with.

Bibliography

Anderson, Lynn. *They Smell Like Sheep: Spiritual Leadership for the 21st Century.* Brentwood, TN: Howard, 1997.

Anyabwile, Thabiti. *Finding Faithful Elders and Deacons.* Wheaton, IL: Crossway, 2012.

Bingham, Nathan W., and Burk Parsons. "What Is the Difference Between Pastors, Elders, and Overseers?" *Ask Ligonier* (podcast), July 27, 2023. https://learn.ligonier.org/podcasts/ask-ligonier/what-is-the-difference-between-pastors-elders-and-overseers.

Dever, Mark, and Jonathan Leeman. *Baptist Foundations: Church Governance for an Anti-Institutional Age.* Nashville: B&H Academic, 2015.

Encyclopædia Britannica. "John Emerich Edward Dalberg Acton, 1st Baron Acton: Quotes." https://www.britannica.com/quotes/John-Emerich-Edward-Dalberg-Acton-1st-Baron-Acton.

Harvey, Dave. *The Plurality Principle: How to Build and Maintain a Thriving Church Leadership Team.* Wheaton, IL: Crossway, 2021.

Hayes, Adam. "Word-of-Mouth Marketing: Meaning and Uses in Business." Investopedia, Sept. 26, 2025. https://www.investopedia.com/terms/w/word-of-mouth-marketing.asp.

Maxwell, John. "Leader-Vision: How to See and Sculpt the Future." Transcript. *Maxwell Leadership Podcast*, Nov. 17, 2021. https://www.maxwellleadership.com/podcast/john-maxwell-leader-vision-how-to-see-and-sculpt-the-future/.

Merkle, Benjamin. *40 Questions About Elders and Deacons.* Grand Rapids: Kregel, 2008.

Merriam-Webster Dictionary. "Polity." https://www.merriam-webster.com/dictionary/polity.

Newton, Phil. "How to Pastor One Another on a Plural Eldership." Founders Ministries, May 2, 2017. https://founders.org/2017/05/02/how-to-pastor-one-another-on-a-plural-eldership/.

———. *The Mentoring Church: How Pastors and Congregations Cultivate Leaders.* Grand Rapids: Kregel, 2017.

Newton, Phil, and Matt Schmucker. *Elders in the Life of the Church: Rediscovering the Biblical Model for Church Leadership.* Wheaton, IL: Crossway, 2014.

Rinne, Jeremy. *Church Elders: How to Shepherd God's People Like Jesus.* Wheaton, IL: Crossway, 2014.

Robert, Henry M., III, et al. *Robert's Rules of Order, Newly Revised.* 12th ed. New York: PublicAffairs, 2020.

Smethurst, Matt. *Deacons: How They Serve and Strengthen the Church.* Wheaton, IL: Crossway, 2021.

Sullivan, Marissa Postell. "Debunking the Myths: Ministry Burnout and Leaving the Ministry." Lifeway Research, July 15, 2025. https://research.lifeway.com/2025/07/15/debunking-the-myths-ministry-burnout-and-leaving-the-ministry/.

Strauch, Alexander. *Biblical Eldership: An Urgent Call to Restore Biblical Church Leadership.* Colorado Springs, CO: Lewis & Roth, 1995.

Thielman, Frank. *Ephesians.* Baker Exegetical Commentary on the New Testament. Ada, MI: Baker Academic, 2010.

Towner, Philip. *The Letters to Timothy and Titus.* The New International Commentary on the New Testament. Grand Rapids: Eerdmans, 2006.

Weisholz, Drew. "Michael Jordan, Mia Hamm Appear in Remake of Iconic 'Anything You Can Do' Commercial." Today, Mar. 15, 2021. https://www.today.com/food/michael-jordan-mia-hamm-return-remake-1997-gatorade-commercial-t211752.

Wiesner, Jeff. "Why Pastors Should Submit to Each Other." 9Marks, Sept. 30, 2022. https://www.9marks.org/article/why-pastors-should-submit-to-each-other/.

www.ingramcontent.com/pod-product-compliance
Lightning Source LLC
LaVergne TN
LVHW020632100826
845148LV00012B/2147
* 9 7 9 8 3 8 5 2 5 5 1 2 2 *